rude awakening:
a mixtape

rude awakening: a mixtape

natalie windle fell

THE UNBOUND PRESS

ISBN: Ebook 978-1-913590-16-1
ISBN: Paperback 978-1-913590-15-4

The Unbound Press
www.theunboundpress.com

Hey unbound one!

Welcome to this magical book brought to you by The Unbound Press.

At The Unbound Press we believe that when women write freely from the fullest expression of who they are, it can't help but activate a feeling of deep connection and transformation in others. When we come together, we become more and we're changing the world, one book at a time!

This book has been carefully crafted by both the author and publisher with the intention of inspiring you to move ever more deeply into who you truly are.

We hope that this book helps you to connect with your Unbound Self and that you feel called to pass it on to others who want to live a more fully expressed life.

With much love,

Nicola Humber

Founder of The Unbound Press
www.theunboundpress.com

to my ancestors —

i'm taking this torch to the finish line.

contents

foreword

humanity needs an upgrade. a major one.

we are headed nowhere fast. we're all stuck in the same old patterns, the same old boring lives, the same old exhausting drama. we're working jobs that betray our souls. we're in relationships with people who are so wrong for us. we fight for causes that are backed by corruption. we feel chained to obligations that feel like prison sentences. we live in cookie-cutter templates that make us feel like we're actors in some grand show. we feel like society controls our destinies.

some of us have no boundaries — we're doormats. some of us have impenetrable walls and have let our hearts freeze over. we're broken, beaten down, and tired. we act like nothing bothers us during the day and numb ourselves with anything that makes the pain go away at night. we spend our money trying to keep up with impossible lifestyles, because that's what we're inundated with every time we pick up our phones, turn on the TV, or fire up our laptops. we don't even know who we are as individuals anymore because we're constantly being bombarded with examples of how to be anything but our true selves.

the world around us is evolving at such a rapid pace. we have access to technology that just a generation ago, we were making sci-fi movies about. and the time gap in between inventions and leaps in innovation gets smaller and smaller by the hour. we're living in a world where we can think about something we want and, with less energy than it takes to stand up, we can have it at our doorstep within days, hours even. we're developing artificial intelligence so intimidating, it's causing an entire body of intellectuals to dedicate their careers to studying what would happen if it replaced the current human workforce.

but yet, here we are. suffering from the same mundane problems that have plagued human beings for EVER. "where's the technology that can help me stop cheating on everyone i'm in a relationship with? where's the app that tells me the exact time i'll be ready to quit my job and finally live out my dreams? where is the button that stops me from feeling like a victim of my circumstances?"

what if i told you that this technology exists? would you believe me? would you think that it's too good to be true?

it's not.

we are living in an unprecedented era. a time when the universe is really trying to help us out because — for lack of a better phrase — we're fucking this whole earth experience up. BIG TIME. so our inner technology is getting a major upgrade, courtesy of the powers that be.

people all over the world are waking up from what feels like the slumber of the century — slumber of the millennium and beyond, even. every day, more and more, little by little, people are starting to question whether or not the life they're living is something they need to settle for. they're starting to think about a way out of the trap. the questioning increases, and increases, and then it starts to evolve into daydreams and plans. and although those plans might make them feel crazy, i assure you they are not. they are just receiving a giant download from the universe.

and it's the most precious gift they may have never asked for. i know i didn't ask for it when it all hit me.

there is a new energy that's flooding our planet. an energy that, if you pick up the signals, will put you on a path to living the way you were truly meant to live. and you don't need any special outer technology to access it. you have everything you need inside of you to tune in. your equipment might be a little rusty, but you can absolutely turn it on and get it working again perfectly. you just need to be willing to install the system update. AND wait patiently while it completes.

and a big part of this update contains sort of a street sweeper. a ravenous, hungry vacuum that wants to take away everything about you that isn't authentic. it takes it all away so you can see that what's left is the perfect, unique, amazing you. the cleaning sucks because we're all running this hoarding program that wants to hang on to all of the garbage we don't need anymore. it's time to let the street sweeper take it away.

this new energy doesn't discriminate. it can hit anyone who wants it and you don't have to pay for it. it is free. and it's here. and it's powerful beyond measure.

so you have to ask yourself: how much longer are you going to play this game with an outdated operating system? how many more days are you going to burn through, living a life half lived?

what do you have to lose by readjusting yourself so that you're more in tune to the frequency that is your SOUL?

* * *

i got really sick and tired of what's out there for someone who's newly awakened. you're either pulled into the fluffy new-age stuff that seems like the bandwagon you're supposed to jump on, but then you feel like an asshole if you're not into kundalini yoga and channeling your spirit guides. OR you get sucked down a conspiracy theory rabbit hole with what seems like no emergency rope to climb back up. and all these awakening "authorities" left me always wanting something more. there was an extreme lack of honesty, of transparency into the real, raw, and oftentimes messy side of figuring out who you are. a lack of real language to explain what i was going through without feeling like i needed to crack some secret code. a lack of humanness.

i've always wished there was someone out there just like me who wrote about going through all of this stuff and was HONEST about it. someone who admitted that they still hated people sometimes, even after realizing we are all one. someone who had the balls to talk about how they love a boozy late night out with friends just as much as they love connecting with their higher self. and after years of looking for this mystical unicorn person, i realized it was me the entire time. what a mindfuck.

i wrote this book for all of the real human beings who are going through an awakening and probably have no idea that they're further along than they think. for people who are burned out from the love and light and spiritual ego and just want someone to relate to. for people looking for validation that their gut feelings are right in that no one knows how to get back to who you are better than YOU.

because here's the deal: at the end of the day, the fact that you woke up on this planet is all the confirmation you need that you're on the right path. my mission is to help you understand this until you believe it and LIVE it from the inside out. you ARE doing this the right way because there is no "right way". and i hope that, through my stories, you'll see yourself and find the courage to keep going. to keep waking up to more and more truth and power and love and healing and magic.

all you have to do is knock the dust off your inner GPS, follow that puppy and enjoy the ride.

* * *

this book is the soundtrack to my very real spiritual awakening.

you have an awakening soundtrack, too. it's playing all of the time.

it's in the conversations you're having at the dinner table.

it's the wind in your car when you're driving with the windows down. it's in your boss droning on in a meeting that should have been an email. it's in the sound of you ugly crying at your worst. and in the "i just pissed myself" laughing fit you're having with your friends. everything you experience is a tiny note in the symphony that is your life.

but what good is a song if no one's listening to it?

if there's anything you take away from this book, let it be the importance of learning how to live your life as one giant mixtape of signs from the universe. we're all on this floating space rock to learn. and grow. and pass that on so that everyone has a chance to be a better human.

and to fucking ENJOY it! why we all seem to voluntarily leave that part out of the equation, i haven't a clue. we need to stop.

chill out and tune in. every day is a new opportunity to wake up to who you truly are. and if that currently doesn't get you going like cold brew on an empty stomach, i hope i can be the one to change your mind.

because it's high time you got your upgrade.

wake up *

there's an alarm clock going off.
can you hear it?

it's both silent and loud.
it's both in your face and out of sight.

it's asking you to question your world, the version of it
you're sold.
it's asking you to stop taking things at face value.
it's asking you to pay attention when things don't make sense.

the sound is confusing because it's a song that's not familiar.
it's not a top 40 hit. it's a deep cut.
but it's also a song we've heard before.
an ancient remix we somehow recognize,
encoded in our DNA.

it's trying to get your attention.
it's begging you to undo everything you know to be true
that is false.
it's offering us a chance at freedom.
it's showing us a new way.

it's the alarm to end all alarms. because the universe knows
we're better than this.
we're so much more powerful than we're lead to believe.
we're so much more capable of taking care of our home.

take the risk and wake up.
go deep.
get out of your head.
react from a sustainable place that's below the surface.
make the adjustments.
reclaim your sovereignty.
remember you're a superhero.

remember we are one.
we've always been.
everything else is an illusion.

you are a tourist

i first heard about death cab for cutie in the back room of the abercrombie i used to work at in college.

i worked out on the floor, saying ridiculous things like "hi, have you tried our jeans?" i also had to walk around every once in a while to spray down the mannequins with cologne, so if you were ever wondering why you can smell the store from miles away, there you go. i was also told that if i see any "pretty people", to ask them if they wanted a job.

there was a rumor that all of the good looking people were customer-facing, and the so-so looking people were out of sight — in the stock room, doing the "clean up" or pre-opening/set up shifts. but i never really noticed. the only thing i did notice was that the guys who "kept out of sight" were cool. they always had the best music.

one day they were playing the death cab album "transatlanticism" and i immediately had to ask what it was. in a typical hipster music snob tone, the one guy was like "you've never heard of death cab?" OK, dude. i bought the CD on my break at the sam goodie downstairs and put it on in my car on the way home.

something about it really hit me. i'm clearly a sucker for music that moves me, but i don't think i realized how transformative the 'cab was for me until now. at the time, i was trying to figure out who i was — not that i ever stopped, but i think something about that time really made me start to question where my life was headed.

and it was a subconscious sort of questioning too. the kind that lingers in the back of your mind and comes in the form of mood swings and irrational anger at things you can't explain. a sort of getting sick of certain topics and conversations and people and whatnot. and what came with it was a getting sick of pop music.

i didn't completely abandon drunk party anthems all of a sudden, but i definitely started my quest for deeper meaning in my headphones. i started really getting into indie music after discovering death cab. it reminded me of the music i liked when i was younger, before i traded grungy off-beat alternative for boy bands and mainstream hip hop. it was kind of like a tiny personal musical renaissance.

"transatlanticism" became the soundtrack for maybe one of my most important years. the first song on the album starts out with the line "so this is the new year and i don't feel any different" and, man, i couldn't have summed up how i felt at the time any better. i was riding into the last year of college and was experiencing a sort of existential crisis — my first of what would come to be many. i mean, here i was about to head into what was promised to be the most party-filled, celebratory, coming of age years of my life and i just felt so fucking empty. like i was missing something. like there was so much more but it was so out of reach.

i could go on about this album and how every song has a line in it that punched me straight in the stomach. the take-home message here is that i'm pretty sure it was my first realization of just how powerful music was. and i know that it is for everyone, but it was the first time me and the universe kind of winked at each other, because it was sort of a point of no return for me in terms of questioning what this life is all about.

and how i would continue to go through my life, being woken up by music and lyrics and rhythms and bass running through my body.

* * *

i kind of forgot about death cab for a while after i graduated college. i was too busy trying to keep up with everyone else. getting jobs, trying to walk with my new adult sea legs. too busy to really dive into existential music lyrics as much as i used to. i had my blinders on.

besides, being that emo music girl wasn't really attractive to the yuppie hot business guy crowd AKA the pool that i thought my future husband was in. i was better off bopping along to lady gaga and flo-rida and ke$ha.

and it's funny because, now that i think about it, there's definitely a correlation between how deep whatever music i was into at the time was, and how in/out of touch i was with my spirit. it's almost like…an imaginary friend i'd throw in the closet when i didn't want to explore myself. searching for meaningful indie lyrics went hand in hand with me searching for myself.

it's kind of like…when you care about yourself, you eat better. you don't watch as much bullshit on TV and you read more books. haha, i don't even know if that makes sense.

anyway, i hit what i'd like to call my "quarter-life crisis" at 25-26 and everything came to a screeching halt in what felt like overnight. i realized i was living a life that wasn't mine. a pop music soundtrack superficial cookie-cutter life with no substance. and it was eating me alive.

i literally felt like i wanted to crawl out of my skin.

i didn't want to be a stay at home mom. i didn't want to have catholic babies and be a pretend catholic. i didn't want to fake smile until my face hurt, having small talk at family functions until i wanted to kill myself. i didn't want a superficial life without meaning.

and so i began my quest, my hero's journey. it was boozy and wild and chaotic and hellish. but it was liberating, soul-nourishing, and true.

i started branching out and making some new friends. started going to offbeat hangouts and concerts, started to really get back into indie music. i remember how much i loved it and, man, there was some **REALLY** great shit out there. and thanks to (now legal) streaming services and things like soundcloud etc, it was so easy to get blissfully lost in a sea of unheard-of artists who all had just as much potential to move the dead energy out of me as the greats. if not more.

over the summer of my quarterlife crisis, a friend invited me to a party boat ride on the schuylkill river one night. after i stepped on, grabbed a local craft beer, and got comfy, the music started.

one song came on and i was like "holy shit, is this DEATH CAB?" and the friend who brought me was like "oh yeah, they just put out a new album" — get the fuck out of here, how did that slip my radar? i guess just like a lot of things, i wasn't paying attention.

the song was "you are a tourist" and it's essentially about this burning in your heart that won't leave you alone. and how it's OK for you to embrace it, let it grow. to not be scared of it, how there's nothing to fear. it was almost like ben gibbard fucking KNEW what i was going through and saved this song just for me, saved the perfect lyrics for when i'd renew my DCFC wonderment.

there's a group of lines in the middle of the song (where the title comes from) that rang through me like pure unadulterated truth. it was almost like my higher self stepping in, holding my hand. it's a simple message that lets you know that if you feel like you're a tourist in your own life, then it's time to make a change. there are so many places you can call home. and then it goes on to tell you that if you're a villain in your own story, go ahead and re-write it.

i mean, fuck.

shortly after this boat ride, i moved out of my parents'

house and into the city. i literally picked up and physically changed my destination. even though i didn't move far away, the depth of what that move meant and still means to me is something unparalleled.

i did feel like a fucking tourist in my own life. and i was exhausted. i craved ownership of my own soul. and i wouldn't rest until i could sit and read my own story, let out a huge sigh, and smile knowing that i wasn't the bad guy anymore. i was my own savior.

* * *

as i get further and further into my awakening, my horizons expand. i consider possibilities for my life that i never would have thought about during that quarter-life crisis. and it feels so so good. the untapped potential and possibilities feel like home now because i am really starting to understand that if i dream something, it's achievable.

one of those dreams is to move out west. my husband and i talk almost daily about picking up and heading out to arizona, a place that has called me to go back ever since my first time there. it's magical and ancient and holds so many codes for me, it's hard to explain. i know that place is somewhere i need to go and spend a part of my life. a place where i can go to grow and learn and wake up to new chapters of life and love and spiritual strength.

and while i don't necessarily feel like a tourist in my life anymore, i do know that it comes in waves. and i know there will be a time when that very distinct feeling of "it's time to go" will find me again. it used to scare me, but now it makes me laugh.

feeling like a tourist is such a gift. feeling like you have no idea who you are or why you're here or what it all means is such an exciting part of life. there's really truly nothing to fear if you embrace it.

and sure, what comes after you embrace it oftentimes looks like chaos, destruction, crumbling. but nothing gets built without some sort of excavation. you have to clear the land to set up a proper foundation. and you have to build brick by brick with so much love and care, so that when it's finished, you will know you're home.

miss independent

i've always been independent. i am stubborn as fuck, a true taurus. i have such a huge problem with authority that my husband jokes i'll undoubtedly get arrested if we ever head into some kind of dystopian police state. i hate being told what to do, even with a looming threat of being thrown into the gulag.

i tested my boundaries as much as i could, and when i couldn't, i rebelled. and i know it's part of growing up and most people go through phases, but i feel like being an independent rebel is drilled into my core.

i graduated college in 2007. i couldn't wait to get out. i had a blast, but i was so ready to work. have my own money. do my own things. i was ready for the next level of freedom that i was told was coming. i welcomed the day when i got my diploma and was ushered into "the real world". and then i got a job.

i remember driving to work every morning, bright-eyed and bushy-tailed, blasting tunes out of my green ford focus hatchback AKA "the turtle". i remember when the morning commute felt like a sort of playing house. getting morning coffee with the rest of the adults just felt so…adult! i didn't notice that, umm, none of them were as happy as i was and were probably dead inside, but i'd come to realize that on my own eventually. and i would die inside too.

but anyway, i loved this new-found feeling of independence. getting paychecks that left a cushion in my bank account. being able to buy things that i couldn't afford as a college student. starting a 401k. i was steadily moving down the laundry list of post-college first job initiation rites. and loving it.

ne-yo's "miss independent" was my morning commute anthem for what i'm pretty sure was most of 2008/2009. i'd bop my head and scream out the lyrics, making sure everyone knew i had "my own thing". i was still living with my parents, and they bought me my car, but HEY no one knew that but me. and besides, i was working hard to climb that damn corporate ladder.

i had broken up with my college boyfriend shortly after we graduated and i was basking in this "miss independent" worldview. i dreamed of being so independent and wealthy on my own that i'd never have to depend on some dude. i'd find a strong man just like ne-yo's persona in the song who would be SO attracted to my mortgage and my manicured nails that set the pedicure off. oh, and my bills are paid on time, too — wanna sleep with me?

it sounds ridiculous now, but i literally couldn't get it out of my head. when we'd go out to the bar, i'd sit there doing that thing where i'd covertly scan the room for prospects and, when i caught them looking at me out of my peripheral vision, i'd straighten up on my stool, toss my hair, maybe play with the straw in my drink, strike up some kind of fake conversation with whoever was next to me, and hope some dude would come over to me.

you know, so i could brag to them about how…independent i was. so i could flex on them with my psychology degree and wax intellectual until they fell on the floor in awe. so i could make them say things like "oh my god, how are you so beautiful and independent and down to earth and cool?" so they could get a raging boner over my independence and take me home. because that's what ne-yo said.

i carried this miss independent persona with me throughout my corporate career, in and out of relationships, and really everywhere else. and it was really fun for a while. until it wasn't.

because the god honest truth about being miss independent is — it just wasn't fucking sustainable. it wasn't realistic. i felt like i was fed a fantasy, brainwashed into thinking doing everything myself was powerful. an unreasonable reaction to the oppression a lot of women in past generations might have felt being forced to get married out of high school and have babies when maybe that wasn't their path after all.

I felt like a lot of us were sold a lie. miss independent might as well be a disney character. she's a seductress of an archetype we can choose to adopt when belle and ariel and jasmine just don't do it for us anymore.

and i can't speak for everyone when i say that i was semi-ruined by the miss independent mythos, but i will fully step into the light on this one, grab a mic, and affirm:

"i enjoy being dependent."

not fully dependent, let me make that real fucking clear. i don't think i'll ever be **OK** with authority. but i enjoy depending on people.

* * *

human beings are communal creatures. we thrive when we're together. we're co-creators. no one person holds all of the wisdom in this world. and while it's very possible to survive on your own and do it all yourself, let's be honest — it feels like shit.

i used to think that independence was the cream of the crop attribute to have and, once i was fully out on my own, i'd be this godly person who was the envy of everyone. the picture of what it meant to be a young modern woman. and even though it seems like we still glorify this persona and are on a trajectory to turn it into the gold standard, i've hung up my hat.

it sucks to be so stubborn that you don't let anyone else help you, which is exactly where my embodiment of "miss independent" led me. i felt so lonely, so overwhelmed. even in relationships, i wouldn't let my guard down so that someone could take care of me. the thought of it used to make me cringe. until i realized that you can only play this part for so long until you crack.

and yes, there are very happily independent women out there. for some, it might just be their calling, their path. but it's not everyone's, make no mistake about it. ne-yo's anthem for me wound up being just another pop song full of empty promises.

in my marriage now, and most of my other (good) relationships, my attraction came from my empathy. my ability to put myself into the other's shoes. my ability to hold space for problems when they felt like they had nowhere else to go.

my husband and i are a team. when i fuck up, he's there. when i need support, he's there. and i accept it lovingly because i know that i can't do it all on my own. i tried and it made me downright miserable. i love having someone there to take the blow for me when i can't fight anymore. i love having a partner that tells me to relax and put my feet up like it's no problem, even though my to-do list is longer than a CVS receipt. i love him because he lets me be independent in spirit, which actually requires a fuck ton of support.

calling it quits on "miss independent" feels bittersweet, but mostly sweet. i truly believe that the world can heal little by little if we just admit that we need each other, on so many levels. we COULD do it all by ourselves, but why should we? we know we don't have to. and for all of the independent people out there: i know you get your kicks from being needed. why not try needing others for a change?

it doesn't make you weak, not at all. in fact, i've recently come to the conclusion that admitting you can't hack it as a free agent is actually amazingly strong. it's vulnerable and real and raw. it's authentic. it's your natural state.

don't be afraid to need someone. don't be afraid to ask for help. don't freak out if you realize you're not as independent as you thought you were. no one's keeping score here. cut yourself a break. find someone who loves you and let them care for you, whether that be family, friends, or a lover. you're only as strong as you are when your needs are fully met.

accept help. the universe wants you to have it so badly.

virtual insanity

technology is amazing. it helps us do amazing things. it helps supplement our clumsy humanity with the aid of something smarter. something more orderly, more streamlined. and we can't get enough of it.

new tech is coming out at a rapid-fire pace. and while there are many things that have made my life easier, i look at where this is going and it freaks me the fuck out. i mean, have you seen "black mirror"? my first reaction to it when it came out was, "hmm, that's really not all that farfetched, i could totally see that happening." and now that some of those episodes ARE happening, i am hashtag disturbed.

jamiroquai's "virtual insanity" came out in the late 90s, and (i THINK) was actually the very first CD that ever entered our home. my dad bought it and then i inherited it soon after. i think i "borrowed" it after i got my five disk CD changer for my 13th birthday because you can't leave any of the slots empty if you want to make sure you get the full effect.

i heard "virtual insanity" again on the radio not too long ago, and it was ironically on a day when i was really getting into what transhumanism is. the formal definition is "the belief or theory that the human race can evolve beyond its current physical and mental limitations, especially by means of science and technology," which on the surface SEEMS like a great thing, right? i mean, don't we want to push our boundaries in the name of a more convenient life?

i don't know. something about the whole thing just really creeps me out. and i won't even get into the spiritual ramifications the transhumanist movement can have on our evolution as humans. scary stuff, to put it extremely lightly. do some research if you're curious.

anyway, i decided to reminisce on my life thus far as it relates to technological advancements, since i really do feel like everyone in my generation has such a unique perspective. we were born into a world that gen z would most surely consider the stone age, came of age along with silicon valley, and are now on the brink of what could quite possibly be a technological tipping point.

* * *

i remember what it was like to live without the internet. i remember what it was like to live without cell phones. without a constant barrage of information hitting your brain every five seconds. i remember a time when you didn't have to know what was going on in the world if you didn't pick up something called a "newspaper", or tuned into the evening news on TV.

i remember a time when you could come home from a hard day of being bullied and feel like you were safe because they couldn't touch you like they can today through social media. i remember when i was free to be an innocent child who didn't feel like they needed to emulate over-sexualized celebrities because i saw them all the time. i remember what it was like to grow up with parents who weren't filming everything. who didn't treat me like i was a pawn in the never-ending reality show that is their instagram life. i remember what it was like to be a kid whose life, for the most part, went blissfully undocumented, save the family photo albums full of pictures from truly memorable events.

i remember what it was like to actually have to call someone to tell them how i felt. use my actual voice. i remember what it was like to have to be extremely courageous and vulnerable in sharing my opinions because i actually had to do it with my mouth, my body. my true self. i remember what it was like to have to stand up to someone attacking my character by facing that person head-on. in person. and i remember how great it felt that i stood up for myself. it strengthened me.

i remember what it was like to live in a world where people didn't die in "texting while driving" car accidents.

i remember what it was like to have to actually go to a library to do research for school projects. i remember having to page through actual books (made of paper) to find the answers to things. i remember living in a world where i didn't have god in my pocket or purse.

i remember living in a world where a night out with friends was spent in one hundred percent presence. a world where we shared each other's deepest thoughts and talked about what it all meant without posting it on the internet. i remember taking pictures with a disposable camera and rushing to the drugstore to get them developed. i remember looking at most of the pictures and loving how i looked in them. i remember looking at the pictures and seeing a great time versus how bad i need to retouch my face. or wishing there was a filtered overlay.

i remember what it was like to not have to worry about a predator trying to talk to me through a direct message on social media. i remember when "don't talk to strangers" applied to being out in public, not while i'm sitting on my couch.

i remember what it was like to be perceived as the person i am. i remember the freedom of what it was like to not have to curate some version of myself to "sell" to the rest of my social media audience. i remember a world where people either said what was on their mind or didn't, and that when they did, it was mostly backed in integrity, not ego.

i remember living in a world where you could have a public meltdown without it being caught on camera. i remember when you could have a bad day without it winding up on twitter. i remember when you could apply for a job and not have to wonder what your employer would be able to find out about you online. i remember what it was like to exist in this world without a "personal brand".

i remember a simpler world.

one that didn't stunt our communication skills. one that

was sort of a level playing field for us all to test out our growth without it going viral. one that thrived on genuine human thinking versus whatever was pushed by whoever screamed the loudest and made it the most catchy.

and through all of this remembering, i can't help but wonder…have we really advanced as much as they're telling us we have? or have we regressed?

and you can call me an old fart, but i truly wish we could go back to that simpler world. i'm not so sure i want to live in a world much more technologically advanced than this one. what else will we lose in the name of artificial intelligence?

will we forget how to do things that used to come naturally? will we become so dependent on our siris and alexas that we make ourselves obsolete?

there's a book called "the circle" by dave eggers (it was also made into a movie) that talks about a big tech company — i think it's supposed to be google or facebook, the likeness is there. cliff notes/take-home message: said big company takes tech to such an insane level that some people don't want it to go any further. and they can't escape it. so they move to the woods.

when i first read that book in 2013, i was like "shit, if that ever starts to happen, i'd be in the woods too," never thinking i'd see a world like that.

except it's here. and it only took seven years.

i am all for tech that helps us. but i can't help but wonder if we already have all we need. i'm thinking we do. as we dive further and further into AI, i find myself wanting to detach. retreat back to who i am as a human. i hate feeling like we're all depending on goddamn robots.

like i mentioned in the death cab chapter, my husband and i have plans to move away from the big city someday (sooner rather than later). we've reached a point where we're overwhelmed. we see what's happening and constantly crave that simpler world we grew up in. it makes me so sad that it's all just a memory and that kids today will never know what it's like to live without everything we have now. but we can make a commitment to not lose our values when tech comes around to try and take them away from us. i know i'm committed to that.

because none of us can appreciate how much easier tech is making our lives if it's simultaneously making us go insane. and i plan on staying conscious and grounded enough to catch myself before i fall victim. human beings are capable of so much more than we think. maybe it's time to tap into the magic inside our DNA instead of handing the power over to the AI overlords.

or maybe it's time to head for the woods.

freedom '90

i had such anxiety getting on that plane to atlanta. i was heading to a client event for my firm and it was the literal last place i wanted to be. i really wanted to be anywhere else. like even the bottom of a coachella port-o-potty.

my firm fired the event planner and then shipped all of her job duties off to me, and if you've worked in corporate america then you KNOW you have no say in this situation. it happens all the time. congratulations, here's double the work at the same price! and you don't complain.

i was actually pretty good at planning events, considering i had no fucking experience whatsoever. and parts of the planning process were amazing. one time i got a free trip to napa to "check out the venue". we were wined and dined so hard. took a tour of a winery and went into the wine cave at stag's leap cellars, which is totally a place where i could see an urn of my ashes hanging out for the rest of time. also, the sales team would always send my co-workers to the events to help schmooze and we would ALWAYS party on the company dime. i miss the hammered ritz carlton lobby convos at 2am about how we all hated our jobs but loved each other.

but most of the event planning process sucked. everyone involved was so hard to please. i cringed every time i'd go to an event because nothing was ever good enough.

someone didn't like the way the fucking seats were arranged in the room, or the buffet didn't have the right butter shapes or something absolutely ridiculous. one guy actually put on his feedback form that he was upset there was no ranch dressing available. and there would ALSO be a client who would buy some top-shelf liquor, drink it all night, and then i'd have to show the bill to my boss and tell him we broke the budget.

and all of this was on top of my other job, which i wasn't really a fan of either. i just didn't want to do anything for this company anymore. or really any company.

* * *

i got to atlanta and headed to the first night's cocktail reception. i'd planned it at the nice steakhouse that was recommended to me. we had really great food, great wine — fantastic wine. the space was a little less than ideal but it worked. i was so tired. i was really good at mingling and ass kissing but it took everything out to me. especially because i knew that these people who were getting my grand performance were the biggest scumbag mooches on the planet and would never buy our products.

one lady wandered in pretty late and was looking around like she'd never seen a restaurant before, so i walked over to her. i put on my face-hurting fake smile and asked her if she wanted something to drink. she was so fucking rude and gave me a line like "well what IS there?" and i had to be all like "oh haha! oh let me get you a menu!" so she picked a damn drink and i walked away. then, i looked over and saw her looking at the food like she'd never seen food before. i walked over to see if she needed a plate (or a fucking new haircut) and when i got over to her, she looked me dead in the eyes with THE most disgusted face.

she gestured over at the food and went, "is THIS all?"

i was like, "yeah it's just cocktails and apps. this is a welcome reception and tomorrow's the dinner", except i probably really said it like a yakked up disney princess in the name of schmoozing. and she huffed and puffed and stormed off to the corner, saying "i thought it was dinner tonight" and then started making some calls, i guess to leave.

and then i just lost it.

i felt a lump in my throat that was the seed of one of those ugly cry beanstalks that flies up and out of your mouth and all over your face and NOTHING can stop it.

i ran to the bathroom — thank god it was just a room for one person. and i sat on the floor. and i cried. and cried. and cried.

why was i even here? i fucking hated it. and i knew i hated it. i was so tired of being trapped. burned out from pretending i even remotely liked my job. so tired of selling my soul for a paycheck and an upward rung on my resume and linkedin contacts. i was so tired from living a double life.

i got myself together as much as i could but i looked in the mirror at my puffy eyes and said "fuck" out loud. i went back out. people asked me if i was OK even though they knew i wasn't. but i pulled myself together enough to down several additional cocktails to take the edge off and talk to some sleazy douchebags until it was time to go back to the hotel.

but once i was back in my hotel, i broke down again. ugly cried so loud and hard. just sat on the bed for what felt like an hour until i finally stopped. i picked up my phone to text my now husband about what was going on. and i started looking for a song to put on, something that would pick me up a little bit. and i found george michael's "freedom '90".

the song was michael's "fuck you" to the music industry. he felt like he couldn't be himself and he was over it. he hated stardom, hated that he couldn't show any authenticity. he wasn't just the hot dude from WHAM! he was so much more.

and the music video? iconic. chock full of supermodels and this smoky room with everyone lip-syncing the lyrics. and then there's the symbolic burning of that jukebox and michael's leather jacket. the burning away of everything that wasn't the real george. and i mean, WHAT an anthem.

i started listening to "freedom '90" in my hotel room. i started to switch my mental state from being a helpless victim to finally seeing a way out. i felt myself fill up to the brim with hope and then just had this intense cathartic release of every shitty reason why i thought i had to stay. i didn't have to stay anywhere. no one does.

i felt like i was being held by something bigger than me. by someone who believed in me and loved me so much. someone who gave me full permission to live the life i was born to live. my higher self.

i finished out the rest of the event and went home to philly. got changed as soon as i got to my apartment, opened up the french doors off the living room, and called my boss. and i quit. put my two weeks' notice in. just like that.

when i hung up, i filled out an application for a personal loan. a giant one. i was approved. figured i'd use it until i figured out what the fuck i was going to do next. and that was that.

i never looked back. never had any regrets. did i wind up becoming an overnight millionaire off some internet marketing scheme like i originally planned? no. did i rack up an insane amount of debt on self-development programs? yes. do i have any idea where my life is going from here? no.

and know that you don't have to know jack shit about anything before you quit. the only thing required for you to be able to leave anywhere is your knowing that you don't belong there. that you're meant for so much more. that your soul wouldn't bug you constantly unless it was trying to tell you something important.

because it's always talking to you.

* * *

i knew pretty early on that i hated corporate america. i encountered really everything that would continue to eat away at my insides within my first like two years of working.

i realized a lot of corporate women acted worse towards each other than in high school. that everyone was always on some fad diet they read about in a tabloid, and were always fucking squirrely whenever it was someone's birthday. "oh, i'm being GOOD today, just a small piece of cake for me!" and they'd fucking cut like a corner of donut off and leave the rest. i can't even type this out right now without going into a small fit of rage over that absolute NONSENSE.

i realized that the raises and bonuses you got were never as high as you thought they'd be. that your promised career path never came to fruition. that the feeling of rotting away in your cubicle is a mostly universal phenomenon.

in the industry i was in, i realized that men either tried to be your dad or tried to fuck you, the older ones anyway. or they talked to you like you had one brain cell, like you were less than. and that sometimes they pity you for being single at 29 and suggest you freeze your eggs, because it's something great to do for yourself, you know? plan for the future. dead serious, that actually happened to me.

i realized that a lot of people sitting at their desks were hungover, just like me. that they sometimes sat at their

ntire day without doing any actual work, just
lized that the people who took long lunches
t real, and those were the ones you should be
friends with. the ones who had all the wisdom on how to
try to play along in corporate america without wanting to
go home and put a metal fork into an electrical socket.

and i existed in this corporate world that i knew i hated,
but i didn't believe in myself enough to give it up. i did it
for ten years. ten long, soul-eroding years. i would leave
one job after i'd had enough for a new job with more pay
and maybe more conveniences, thinking that eventually i'd
make enough money to be cured of that nag in my
stomach. cured of the handicap of not being able to just
happily sit at a desk for eight hours and collect my reward.

but you can't cure your soul. it can't be outsmarted.

even though it seems like i quit my job in a hurry, the
wearing away of my soul was a slow burn. you don't want
to admit to yourself that you aren't the crazy one. this
office really IS fucked up. these people really ARE
sociopaths. you really ARE being mistreated. because
every time you feel that way, there's always someone who
will try to make you feel better by saying things like, "oh,
it's just how it is". i would look at people who genuinely
looked like they enjoyed their jobs with an intense jealousy.
i imagined them waking up in the morning, making their
coffees, kissing their spouses and babies and waving to
them as they pulled out of their driveways, whistling.

i wanted that to be me so badly. i wanted to be able to play the game, because it's easier to play the game than to try to exist outside of it. i mean, it is by design. it's difficult to start your own business, even harder to keep it alive. the people who quit their jobs without anything else lined up are almost always looked at like they're mentally ill.

when i was first starting out in recruiting, someone more senior than me taught me how to read resumes. and by read resumes, i mean read them like they do on the OTHER side — how to read them as an employer. things that would immediately disqualify someone? a gap between jobs more than one year. length of job less than one year. changes in careers (lack of consistency). and don't even think about hiring someone who seems overqualified, because they'd be bored. and throw away anyone living more than 20 miles away from the office.

if any of these things stuck out at me, i'd trash the resume. without knowing anything real about the person. and i read resumes like this for a really long time as i was hiring people. where's the room for being human here? reading that all back seems ridiculous to me now.

i met some of my best friends at my jobs. i met my husband at a job! i constantly think about how many friends i might have thrown away, how many people i missed out on meeting and loving. but that's neither here nor there.

* * *

to anyone reading this who felt their arm hair stand on

end. who felt their stomach flip flop because you know this is you too. to anyone reading this who wants to stop selling their soul to the devil, listen to me:

just go for it. really, just do it.

i am not going to ramble on about how the universe will take care of you, or how your dreams are just a positive affirmation away. there's enough of that out there. and it's not based in reality.

the reality is that it will be hard. you will fumble through what you're supposed to be doing next. you will think you get it so many times and fall — hard. you'll second guess yourself every single day. you'll endure family and friends alternating between thinking you're a legend and questioning your sanity.

the reality is that the odds for living outside the system aren't stacked in your favor. it's counting on you to stay in it forever. or at least until you expire AKA retire. they want you to stay in it and give it your all until you're used up, too old. then, and only then, can you really enjoy life, enjoy freedom. only then can you travel, write that book, sleep in and do nothing. and bet against the odds that you'll probably need to use your retirement funds to get your hip replaced. or maybe your knee. and your wife's knee. and hip. maybe both of them.

and it sounds crazy putting it that way, but it's the truth. a hard one. a harsh reality.

so the question you need to ask yourself isn't, "what am i

going to do next?" it's "how much longer can i take this?"

the question isn't, "how am i going to afford it?" it's, "how am i going to authentically stay in a place that i know is wrong for me?"

it's not "how can i find ways to stick it out until i figure out that great business idea?" it's "how will i be able to continue lying to myself when my soul is screaming at me?"

these are the real questions. the ones that make you sick, but sick in that way when you ask yourself a cold-hearted truth. the truth doesn't always feel good. in fact, most of the time it feels like shit. but what's on the other side is a freedom unparalleled.

while things may not be easy for you when you take the leap, they will always be true. your soul wouldn't be tapping you on the shoulder with increasing frequency and pressure if you weren't supposed to listen. and even though things won't be easy, you will always be taken care of as long as you have faith. it took me a really long time and a lot of unnecessary struggling to get that through my thick skull. i'm still getting it through.

the act of leaving something that is wrong for you is easy. getting the courage to do it is hard. but go there anyway, go get it. be brave and be the trendsetter you know you are. pave a new road for everyone else to live their truths. be a wayshower.

you only get one shot at making this lifetime one worth living. don't waste another day of it on someone else's dream where you don't have a starring role.

every breath you take

she finally got away from him.

she was his slave. he kept promising her more and more but she was getting less and less. she felt less and less human. all she wanted was enough money to go to massage school. that's how they met too. he conned her into giving him a "massage" after he spotted her reading a book about massage therapy at the country club she worked at.

he whored her out to the elites. he flew her everywhere and anywhere for underage sex with whoever could afford it. he took her teenage years from her. and she just couldn't break away. he made it so hard. so did his best friend, a female partner in crime. they had an entire team of people who were paid to look the other way. an entourage that would rival that of a royal family.

and there were others like her being held against their will. from all over the world, all sorts of backgrounds. a flavor for everyone. captives held in a stable for those who wanted a thrill. a thrill they just don't stop seeking. because the adrenaline from their high-powered lives stop scratching the itch after a while, and so they seek more. more power.

she knew so much, too much. there were pictures of her with high powered people. people who you'd think would know better than to provocatively pose with an underaged girl in a crop top.

his right-hand girl told her that she could attend a massage school in chiang mai if she recruited a girl to bring back for him. she went, it wasn't like she had a choice.

and then she met her knight in shining armor. her savior. he was a trained fighter, the one she'd been praying for, dreaming about. she told him everything. he held her safe. he'd protect her. she just knew, trusted him with her soul. the soul that would risk dying to be set free. her knight told her she didn't have to go back to him. and she didn't.

"have a nice life."

that's all he said when she told him she wasn't returning and was moving to australia with her new husband. and, for a moment, she was free, even though it took her a while to let it sink in. even if the freedom was temporary, it was palpable. real.

and then things started to crumble around her captor. an investigation back home was underway. a young girl's parents discovered his claws in her and reported him to the authorities. their daughter was giving massages in exchange for money from a man who also molested her. pressed her for more and more, promising more and more in exchange. all too familiar.

she panicked, wondering if she was safe in australia. if the new life she was creating would get ripped out from under her just like her high school years. she found out she was named and identified as a victim by someone back home.

she didn't even wonder how they found her. they could

find anyone. the power they had was unfathomable. but they did. they called her at home. first, bonnie.

then clyde. his voice on the other end felt like a taser gun to the throat. he wanted her to tell him everything, and then he wanted her to shut up. he knew where she was, who she was with. he didn't have to say much. but she wasn't going to let him own her again. she was going to talk.

she hangs up the phone, and then "every breath you take" comes on. the first drumbeat is timed perfectly with virginia roberts giuffre hanging up the phone with jeffrey epstein. and then a black screen and the credits. and then the little netflix "next episode" progress bar at the bottom right.

at least, that's how it goes in my head.

* * *

i first found out about the epstein case in 2018, shortly after i discovered like 894723486 different schools of conspiratorial thought at once. i came across a picture of this strange blue and white striped, golden building on this random caribbean island. i was so intrigued, like who wouldn't want to know what the fuck was in there? have you seen it?

and then i fell headfirst into the entire case. the people he was tied to. the girls. the plane. the properties. it was unreal. and how he was somehow still allowed to just saunter through life, hobnobbing with everyone and anyone. starting charitable organizations while he was supposed to be serving jail time. avoiding basically any and all repercussions for some absolutely heinous crimes.

i just couldn't get over it. why wasn't anyone else talking about it? i felt like it was all i COULD talk about. but it's a lot like most other things that come across our attention spans. news has to meet certain criteria to even get put out there, and then it has a shelf life. people forget if it's not constantly being reinforced. and that's when it dawned on me: this was purposely not being reinforced in our consciousness, let alone getting any serious airtime. and that's when i started to see the bigger picture.

i started to remember all of the newsworthy things on this planet that were sensationalized and then forgotten during my lifetime. except for the occasional reminder of the anniversary date, or reference to it in a movie, these things came and left society's radar as fast as we got over big fake tits and bleach blonde hair.

columbine. the oklahoma city bombing. earthquakes in california. hurricane katrina. the OJ trial. casey anthony. lorena bobbitt. jean benet ramsey. all here and gone. even 9/11 became like that for me, unfortunately. it's like the moment these things happen, you're like, "oh there's no way i won't go a day thinking about this." and then, just like the high school breakup you think you'll never get over, it just fades away.

i'm not sure why i got so into the epstein case. maybe it's because i was intrigued by his famous friends and straight-up mystery of how he became connected with them in the first place. maybe it was because i could see myself in all of his victims that came forward, remembering exactly what it was like to be a doe-eyed, people-pleasing teenager, just looking for extra cash. maybe it was because, after a certain point in my awakening, i stopped tolerating things at face value and knew there was always more to a story.

or maybe it was that thing that happened to us in the bahamas while we were on a college spring break trip, sophomore year. that time where we naively got into a limo with a bunch of old guys who said they worked for bacardi. who told us we were invited to a company party with unlimited booze and music. who didn't tell us that we'd be walking into a room full of naked girls who looked just like us. all strung out and standing at the front of a room like they were on display.

"why don't you get up there?" one of them said to me. i looked at him and asked him if he had daughters. he stared at me as if i was speaking a different language. we left shortly after. come to think of it, it's really a miracle that we were even allowed to leave. no clue what these people could have been capable of.

it's a combination of everything.

and then epps gets arrested. i couldn't believe it! it was one of the only conspiracy "prophecies" that came true at the time, and i was floored. and then more started to come out. more victims. more connections. i was following the money. following it so hard that it fucking led me to places where i realized i personally had a kevin bacon degrees of separation connection to epstein. wild as hell.

SO obviously, i was just chomping at the bit for everything to come tumbling down. because that's what the good guys do, right? make sure justice is served. i was finally going to see the biggest criminal in my lifetime get his ass handed to him.

but then i dug more. went deeper. came across some really dark shit that's somewhere between true and unthinkable. eugenics research. wanting to create a perfect race. secretly pulling the strings behind the victoria's secret conglomerate. more shocking connections. ties to some really prestigious institutions.

and that's when i realized that we probably weren't going to see epstein get the level of punishment he deserved. it deflated me. but i was still holding on to the hope that he'd at the VERY least get put away for what he did to all of these teenage girls. THAT at least was very public, and very provable. right? wasn't it? and then all of THAT would eventually maybe lead to frying all of the bigger fish that need to be fried so badly. wouldn't it?

and then this fucker "kills himself". absolutely unbelievable.

but you know what? in this world, it IS believable.

i remember when i found out about it, my GUT REACTION was a calm, collected, "of course he did." and by of course he did, i mean of course he DIDN'T. this guy didn't kill himself. at least not the way everyone thinks he did. there are so many fucking theories, you can literally choose your own adventure here. but bottom line, this "death" stinks.

and, of course, this was sensationalized all over the news. about how the guards maybe like fell asleep. or how something was wrong with the security system (in a supermax prison, that's really reassuring). and how his prison roomie was conveniently…absent. i mean, COME ON. is this a fucked up scooby doo mystery? whose mask do i need to pull off?

are we really that dumb to believe that THIS is what happened to this guy? conveniently right before he was probably going to give up some major names? no one in their right mind could possibly believe what we're expected to believe here. but in the end, it doesn't really matter what we believe when it's not something we think about anymore.

we move on to other sensational news once the manufactured buzz dies down. we're distracted by new news with its own shelf life. lather, rinse, repeat forever and ever.

and, usually, i don't really give a shit. but this one REALLY bugs me. i can't just let this one go. it's a joke with my friends and family now. i'm now the proud owner of an "epstein didn't kill himself" ugly christmas sweater. i repost epstein memes whenever i see them. yeah, it's funny and all, but deep (or not so deep) down, i'm making a point.

we can't just forget about big things that happen that go unsolved, just because they're not on TV anymore. and we can't settle for the watered-down, recycled content put out about cases like this, knowing full well it's not the whole story. there are SO so many things that could get turned around if only enough people stayed on it and pushed it into the hands of the right people. look at "making a murderer". you always hear about a new court case or a new piece of evidence. a new team that wants to take it on for free and help bring justice where it's due.

and while i know steven avery is child's play compared to the pedophile industrial complex known as epstein enterprises, that doesn't mean that the power of keeping important things in the minds of the masses can't change the world. a tall order, i know. but not impossible.

i think about virginia and the other victims and how they must feel as they watch the world in real time learn about, get hyped about, and then forget about the hell they must have lived through. how this guy just destroyed their lives without any remorse. they're the ones i keep epstein in everyone's consciousness for. them and all of the underground others who have no voice.

i scripted that entire phone scene in my head the first time i heard "every breath you take" post-epstein. what that must have felt like to have all of the memories of someone owning you come flooding back. feeling your captor's voice vibrate through you from the other side of the world, feeling like he's making you give one of his "massages". all the times she wanted to leave but couldn't. the blackmail. the other girls.

the song also holds a double meaning for me, in that i'm still watching him. whether he's alive or dead, there is still so much that i'm staying alert for. i keep the hope alive that we're not done yet. there's still so much justice that needs to be served, so much truth that has to come to light.

and it always comes to light.

i was on a picnic with friends a couple of weeks ago and, after three beers, i proclaimed, "the world might have forgotten about jeffrey epstein, but i fucking didn't." and if that's not a total mood to adopt for a cause you care about, then i don't know what is.

truth*

truth is inconvenient.

it's not polite.
it won't ask you if you're ready
before it reveals itself.
it comes without warning.

it is a calm assassin.
it can kill with a single whisper.
it can bring an entire civilization to its knees.
it can illuminate the darkest of secrets
with the tiniest of lights.
it is the most powerful and
most effective weapon that exists.

and yet, we turn it away.
we ignore it.
we refuse its medicine.
we willfully pass it over because
we've evolved into a society that
values comfort over growth.
values superficial order over
the needed chaos of change.
values inauthentic facades of happiness over
core-cutting, cathartic reality.

but the truth doesn't give a fuck about
how you handle it,

or if you can.

it still comes.
and it doesn't rest until it flips over every lie.
eventually, those that run from it get to a cliff
where they have to
turn and embrace it
or make a choice to stay in the dark.
and the choice to stay in the dark
is a death sentence.

your ego hates the truth.
your soul needs it.
we are in a time on this planet where personal
and collective truths are tired of hiding.
and we need to be brave enough to trade
the comfort of our illusions for
the inevitable, uncomfortable truth.

and while it will crumble everything away
we thought we were sure of,
it's only up
from there.

pink houses

growing up, whenever i'd hear "pink houses" by john mellencamp, i thought about flags waving, the fourth of july, safety, prosperity, and freedom. and then, a few years ago, i started hearing something else. during the intro, my mind scripted a slow-moving cinematic display of cars blowing up. dust flying everywhere. people running screaming and scared amidst an apocalyptic hellscape. all while mellencamp strummed along. a slow-mo pan out of the country burning down to a cheerful rock anthem. and i laughed at the image in my mind, because as morbid and fucked up as it looked, it was the truth.

americans, collectively, are just zombies strumming along to the song of patriotism, ignoring the reality of it all. and that's about the most american thing we do. i decided to do some research on mellencamp and "pink houses" and was giddy with joy when i found out me and johnny were on the same page:

> *Mellencamp is from a rural town in Indiana and often writes about the American experience. His songs are sometimes misinterpreted as patriotic anthems, when a deeper listen reveals lyrics that deal with the challenges of living in America as well as the triumphs.*
> *Mellencamp has expressed his love for his country, but has also criticized the US government for going to war in Iraq, developing a dependency on foreign oil and not doing more to support the working class.*

*"It's really an anti-American song," Mellencamp told
Rolling Stone about "Pink Houses." "The American
dream had pretty much proven itself as not working
anymore. It was another way for me to sneak something
in."*

*Inspiration for this song came when Mellencamp was
driving on Interstate 65 in Indianapolis. As described
in the first verse, he saw a black man sitting in a lawn
chair just watching the road. The image stuck with
Mellencamp, who wasn't sure if the man should be
pitied because he was desolate, or admired because he
was happy. (via WIKIPEDIA).*

the opening verse he's talking about on the surface seems
like a happy-go-lucky description of someone who just
happens to live near a highway, but then i started to really
think about it. and the more i thought, the less happy it
got.

how could anyone in their right mind listen to those lyrics
and think that's worth celebrating? but i definitely did for
most of my life. i took the song at face value. i bet before
you started reading this, you thought this song was all
about how we have it so great here in the USA. but do we?
if we're lucky, as americans, we'll get chances to see the
cracks in the disney princess facade we're all sold. getting
screwed on your taxes unexpectedly. losing your business
or job due to economic conditions beyond your control.
having trouble finding work because you fucked around

when you were younger and now have a blip on your permanent record. confusing legal hoops to jump through when you're trying to do something great for yourself and stand up to the man. is that freedom? well, it sure is somethin' to see. and what do we do when these things happen to us? we accept them as our fate. we feel bad for ourselves. we take up the burden of a broken system instead of standing our ground and admitting we deserve better. and this is ironically completely unamerican.

* * *

i currently work at my dad's machine shop in northeast philadelphia. and if you ever want to experience a spotlight illuminating the american mirage, come visit. my drive into work from my apartment closer to the city center has been one of the most eye-opening experiences of my entire life. when i get off i95 and make my way towards work, i'm encountered by people who are anything but thriving. the opioid crisis is extremely evident in this area. the show intervention highlighted the neighborhood for an entire season in 2019. the street i drive down has a teetering addict on just about every corner, and a drug dealer a few blocks away. a prostitute either on her way "home" or just getting out to start the day. somber, struggling business owners opening up their dilapidated storefronts with their fingers crossed, hoping nothing bad happens to them. kids innocently walking through all of this on their way to school. it's a stark contrast.

several times a week at the convenience store where i stop for coffee, i give whatever extra cash i have on me to someone who needs it. and the people who ask don't always look like who you'd think they'd look like. i look into their eyes and i see myself. i think about just how quickly my life would deteriorate if my husband and i lost our incomes, our families couldn't support us, and we had nowhere to go. add in our predisposition to enjoying the occasional substance to take the edge off, and BOOM. it doesn't take much.

one day, i drove by two women having an argument at a bus stop. one of them looked completely strung out on drugs while the other was screaming at her. all while a young child (who couldn't have been older than six) was with them, sat on a bench in tears. on a different day, i was on my way home and a junkie on a hoverboard in the bike lane next to me wobbled off and the board flew under my car. i ran it over, destroying it. i got out of my car to see if the guy was OK and i don't think he even knew where he was or what just happened. to describe him as strung out was an understatement.

at the start of the 2020 pandemic, when they started closing everything down, the line at the local gun shop was blocks long for several days in a row. i have to text my dad every single day when i get home safe. i'm 35 years old. but i don't mind, because i get it. it really is no joke. my dad tells me that when he bought his business in 2006, the area wasn't this bad. it was no beverly hills but people were doing OK. typical middle-class neighborhood. the houses across the street were filled with friendly families. smiling people going to work each day. hardly any violence. but things really took a turn, and fast. every year, the established residents would move. more junkies showed up on the streets. more hookers, fewer businesses. more drugs, fewer families. one morning, my dad got to the shop to find police tape across the driveway. someone was murdered there overnight and now his property was part of a crime scene. the city painted his outside walls with a special substance that makes it hard for graffiti to stick. there's a dedicated task force that comes to clean it up. he doesn't even bat an eye anymore when it happens.

my dad's old secretary spent her entire life in the northeast. listening to her tell stories about what it was like to grow up there is like listening to some make-believe fairy tale. it's so far from what it is today, it doesn't sound at all like the same place. i think about how heartbreaking it is for me to drive through and see what i see every day, but then i think about how hard it must be for her. how they never pictured this happening to their comfortable, quintessentially american neighborhood. i couldn't imagine driving through the neighborhood i grew up in, witnessing it turning into a war zone of sorts. but it's a possibility. it's a possibility for every neighborhood. and that's the problem, isn't it? if the bubble you live in hasn't been touched by this unspoken, yet increasingly common american nightmare phenomenon, you'd have no idea. you could happily live your entire life far removed from whatever sensationalized bullshit you see on the news. "that would NEVER happen here." this is what we say as a collective. americans refuse to see. we love to exist in the false story we're sold that we're the greatest there is. we're untouchable. no one would ever come and hurt MY america! it just isn't possible!

in 2014 went to europe for the first time on a solo trip. i spent time in italy, france, and switzerland. i came home and was like, "shit, america really isn't THAT great." my friend's boyfriend immediately told me i was crazy. maybe it was all the gelato. but i'm not crazy. and i know i'm right.

* * *

as i was researching "pink houses", i realized just how fucked up and warped americans are. there's a track record of high-powered people trying to use "pink houses" as a pro-american anthem when it's the farthest thing from it. and poor mellencamp is there trying to clean up the mess, trying to correct everyone. i've never related to a classic rock icon more (other than springsteen).

> *In 2004, the song was played at events for Senator John Edwards' presidential campaign. The song was also used at events for Edwards' 2008 presidential campaign. (via WIKIPEDIA)*

clearly, john edwards didn't listen to pink houses with a critical ear. or ask mellencamp why he wrote it.

> *"Pink Houses"…was played by Senator John McCain at political events for his 2008 presidential campaign. Mellencamp contacted the McCain campaign pointing out Mellencamp's support for the progressive wing of the Democratic Party and questioning McCain's use of his music; in response, the McCain campaign ceased using*

Mellencamp's songs." (via WIKIPEDIA)

could you imagine what that phone call was like?

> *In January 2009, Mellencamp played "Pink Houses"
> at We Are One: The Obama Inaugural Celebration at
> the Lincoln Memorial. (via WIKIPEDIA)*

THIS one really gets me. really unsure as to why
mellencamp decided to do this, but maybe he was
exhausted from being misunderstood and decided to give
barry o a pass because he liked him? something to keep in
your back pocket.

and, just for shits and giggles:

> *In 2010, "Pink Houses" was used by the National
> Organization for Marriage (NOM) at events opposing
> same-sex marriage. At Mellencamp's instruction, his
> publicist sent a cease and desist letter to NOM stating
> "that Mr. Mellencamp's views on same-sex marriage
> and equal rights for people of all sexual orientations are
> at odds with NOM's stated agenda" and requesting
> that NOM "find music from a source more in harmony
> with your views than Mr. Mellencamp in the future."
> (via WIKIPEDIA)*

are your eyes rolling yet? mine are in the back of my skull.
the conspiracy theorist in me wants to believe that these
politicians and activist groups are trolling the shit out of us,
but the logical side of me thinks it's probably just a
manifestation of our grand american illusion. america is
the best, right? how could you think otherwise?

and here's one more example of just how naive we are:

> *MTV ran a contest based on this song where they gave away a pink house in Indiana. They got a great deal on the place — John Sykes at the network remembers paying $20,000 for it — but unfortunately, the house was across from a toxic waste dump. When Rolling Stone ran an article pointing this out, Sykes flew to Indiana and bought another house, which is the one they gave away (after painting it pink). According to Sykes, the house near the waste dump stayed on the books at MTV until 1992, as they couldn't get rid of it. (via WIKIPEDIA)*

so you mean to tell me that MTV unconsciously recreated the home that mellencamp highlighted in the first verse of "pink houses"? you can't make this shit up.

this happens all the time in america. every single day, we're fed insane amounts of propaganda on how amazing this country is, when in fact, it fucking sucks. don't get me wrong, i am extremely blessed. i have a job. i'm white and educated. i grew up in a great neighborhood. my parents are still together and are two of the greatest people on the planet. but the harsh truth is that i'm not most americans. i'm what most people THINK pink houses is about.

i am writing this after a week of unprecedented times in america. the death of george floyd set off a chain reaction of people starting to wake up to the american illusion, whether they know it or not. many people are angry that we're still dealing with racism. many people are exhausted from being out of work due to the pandemic ripping their livelihoods out of their hands and their loved ones from their families. many are hurt to the core that a police force that's supposed to be our source of comforting safety has been infiltrated by disgusting human beings on the power trip of a lifetime – and who ruin it for all of the good cops.

but you know what rattles me the most? that we're still looking to politicians to save us. that we're still holding out hope that people at the top of our chain are going to bail us out, that they really, genuinely give a shit. that voting in presidential elections is the answer. that taking to the streets will be the thing that changes it all, that we'll finally be heard. voting for candidates like the ones who refuse to take a deep listen to songs like "pink houses". and if they're not listening to that, they're probably not listening to you.

we're going to need to think a lot deeper and harder if we want to actually live in the american environment that we're sold. one of my favorite concepts i learned about in graduate school was chan kim and renee mauborgne's "blue ocean strategy". based around strategic marketing, they highlight that the businesses that do the best are the ones who get out of the over-competitive, saturated "red ocean" markets and make their own unique waves. they create new "blue oceans" that change the landscape and take the world by storm, and a lucrative customer base that's hungry for change along with them. we need to find a blue ocean as americans.

we need to open our eyes to the fact that we'll never win the freedom, safety, and loving country we deserve by repeating history. and while i whole-heartedly believe that everyone who speaks up about causes they believe in has the best of intentions, we need to look at what we can best do to change the system in a new way. and, in my humble opinion, we either need to burn the entire thing down and build on top of it, or completely abandon it and create something new elsewhere. the old templates haven't worked because the universe is challenging us to use a new one.

i'm here to build anew. my spirit won't have it any other way. i love this country, but i love its people even more. because maybe my little pink house is somewhere off the metaphorical grid, holding space for the other little pink houses to come get built around me. and maybe the building will be so contagious that, in the blink of an eye, we're all of a sudden living in the utopia we all deserve. the utopia that is our god-given right. a utopia of the kind of pink houses mellencamp would be proud of. and wouldn't THAT be somethin' to see?

return to innocence

i can't remember how exactly i acquired the "pure moods" cassette tape. i'm not sure if i got it at the wall in the springfield mall or if my mom actually called the 1-800 number and bought it from the TV commercial that was constantly on.

either way, it was my total jam. it was a compilation of all of these new-age, ambient, global songs, and for some reason, i was glued to it. definitely some past life shit. i was nine when it came out.

the first song on it was enigma's "return to innocence", a banger if you've never heard it. it starts with this chant that rips right through you. a man with this booming deep voice melts you into a puddle before any lyrics come in. even as a nine-year-old, i knew it was powerful.

it was also in the closing scene of the (dreamy) jonathan taylor thomas (JTT, swoon) movie, man of the house. chevy chase marries JTT's native american mother and she walks down the aisle with enigma playing.

"return to innocence" for me was one of those songs i'd forget about for years and then, whenever i'd hear it again, i'd go right back to who i was when i first heard it. that little nine-year-old girl who was so moved by the chanting. and each time i heard it as i got older, the more it moved me. every single time.

so it's no surprise to me that now that it's one of the most important songs of my awakening. at 33, it came back to life randomly on my sirius radio channel "90s on 9" and i did one of those laughs that turns into a semi-ugly cry. this time the song moved me to the point where it flat out pushed me off. pushed me into something else. pushed me into a new chapter.

i was SO moved and inspired this time around that it made me fucking leap into an entire business venture, complete with lead magnets and sales pages.

i started to think about the actual lyrics for the first time and not get lost in the hypnotic chanting. i realized that the innocence enigma was talking about was that of the inner child. that innocent, vulnerable, deep part of you that fades away the older you grow. the part that moves so far away that you forget just how powerful you are. the part that gets pushed to the back burner because all the "cool" adult shit you're sold crowds the space. until one day, you wake up and fucking hate yourself.

and i was feeling that, hard-core.

after this realization, i thought people were CRAZY to not get back in touch with their inner child. i mean, why were we all walking around with this blatant untapped potential inside of us and willingly ignoring it? walking around with an invisible genius in our pocket. oh, the absurdity.

i HAD to do something. i HAD to make it my crusade to awaken each and every inner child in the world. through an email course called "the inner child project". for, i think, $49. that i eventually wound up just giving away for free because i realized that it wasn't going to be my ticket to all of the outrageous shit i was trying to delusionally manifest at the time. big sigh.

but i **ALSO** came to the extremely significant conclusion that while the inner child project didn't make any money, it did give me **MY** inner child back. i was ultimately inspired to write it for **ME**. i was really just getting started on my own journey back to myself, and it was everything i didn't know i needed. it was a tangible gift from my higher self to me, post-agreeing to spend the rest of my life becoming awakened.

and now, it's my gift to you. bear in mind that i hadn't yet found my voice when i wrote it. i thought about editing it, rewriting it, but i think it's more powerful to leave it as-is. it was really trippy reading it back to myself after kinda forgetting about it for a couple of years. and it also gives me the deepest appreciation for not giving up on writing just because i felt stuck for so long. i eventually became unstuck, and so can you.

unearthing who you truly are is hard, dirty work. and every time you have concrete evidence that you did it, it's to be celebrated.

so without further ado, please enjoy the inner child project. remember, it was originally written as a daily email course. you'd get an email a day from me for 30 days.

you can read it all at once, once a day, chunks at a time, actually complete the action steps, tell me to go to hell, i don't care. just make sure you read it. your inner child will thank you.

especially if you guys are meeting for the first time.

* * *

DO THINGS BEFORE YOU'RE READY

Children don't think before they do things, sometimes to their detriment. But isn't that also how they learn? When a child who is just starting to walk then starts to run, he will almost certainly fall at some point. That's how he learns to run even better and faster the next time, because he is now learning about the possibilities (good and bad) of what could happen when he chooses to run.

Think about what would happen if he decided to not even try. You probably think that's crazy and laugh at such a nonsense idea. But this is exactly what happens to all of us as adults when we don't try something because we don't have it all figured out.

Your challenge today is to write about something that you've been putting off before you feel ready. Think back to what it must have been like for you when you started walking, or even use the children in your own life as examples to really visualize the process. How could this lesson help you break through?

HAVE NO SHAME

Have you ever looked up the true definition of the word "shame"? When you Google it, the following comes up: a painful feeling of humiliation or distress caused by the consciousness of wrong or foolish behavior.

When children make wrong choices they keep moving forward regardless. It is all part of their learning process. As we grow up, the potential for wrongdoing becomes more and more complex, but that doesn't mean that we ever stop learning from our mistakes. Even the worst offenses have something to teach us. Think about how wonderful the world would be if we all had a child-like mindset when it came to processing a wrong choice. Do, learn, grow.

Today's challenge is to choose one thing in your life that you are ashamed of and look at it with the eyes of an adult trying to show a child the lesson in their mistakes. With complete kindness and lack of judgment, create an affirmation for yourself that will help you turn a shameful experience into a lesson.

TELL IT LIKE IT IS

I remember one afternoon when I went to a friend's house after kindergarten class, her house was really messy and disorganized compared to mine, so I told her mom straight up (I still LOL over this). When I got home, I remember my mom telling me that it wasn't nice to say things like that to people, and she was right. I mean, it's totally impolite to say things like THAT, but that's not my point here.

My point is that at some time in all of our lives, we gave not a single fudge about what came out of our mouths, especially if it was speaking an observable truth. And for many of us (myself included), the ability to do this gets buried under layers of learned insecurity and we trade the freedom of speaking our truths with the comfort of not rocking the boat.

The world needs more boat-rockers, and I know you have at least one place in your life where a ship could use your push. Your challenge today is to think about a situation in your life where you've been holding back speaking a truth that really needs to be heard. Write about it and process what comes up.

BELIEVE

Santa Claus. Mermaids. Monsters. Dragons. Superheroes. Can you remember a time in your life where a huge part of you believed these were real? How excited you were at the possibility of potentially meeting such an individual and how they enhanced your imagination beyond your wildest dreams?

Over time, reality sets in and you slowly begin to see that Santa was just a collective childhood fantasy. Superheroes stay within the pages of comic books, and mermaids stay inside the confines of Disney's "The Little Mermaid"…even though a huge part of me thinks mermaids are out there somewhere!

While you're probably not going to start believing in Santa Claus again any time soon (when you're NOT in front of anyone under the age of 10), I'm guessing when you stopped believing in your childhood fantasies, a part of you stopped believing in real wonders of life. You stopped believing in possibilities that seemed too far out of your reach to be a reality.

Is there something in your life that you've always dreamed about having or doing but stopped believing that it could ever be a reality for you? Your challenge today is to time travel back to who you were when you believed in Superman. The universe really is magnificent and can make dreams come true if you just believe. Work through an issue that's calling your attention.

LOVE UNCONDITIONALLY

Our parents were all far from perfect. They're human beings with human problems and were just trying to get by in life, one lesson at a time. When we were young, our parents could do no wrong. Dad lost his job? You still loved him exactly like you did the day before he got fired. Mom going through depression? You still hugged her and thought the world of her, just as you did the week before when she playfully danced with you at the party. You fought with your siblings and loved them 5 minutes later like it never happened. You loved without a list of conditions.

How many of us quickly write off other people because they're suddenly deemed "hard to love"? How many of us hold back our natural inclination to extend love to someone who needs it, just because it might make us look bad?

There was a time in your life where this wasn't an option because you only knew how to love. Is there someone in your life that you've been holding back your fullest expression of love to because of your own insecurities? Today, send this person your unconditional love. You can send it to them mentally through the universe or you can call or text them if you're so called.

SEEK OUT ENTERTAINMENT / ENTERTAIN YOURSELF

OK full disclosure, I really hated going to church as a kid. Don't get me wrong, I loved God and was super into the church songs sometimes, but I didn't understand anything that was going on until I was old enough to process things. My sister and I were so fidgety and got a lot of side-eye from my parents (except when we caught my dad's eye and made him laugh). My mom would pack crayons and books and baggies of goldfish, but that didn't always hold us over the full 90 minutes. So what did we do? We got resourceful.

We made stuff out of the hymn books in the pews. I used to look at the congregation and try to see whose yawns were making other people yawn. I used to count how many times the priest would use Catholic buzz words (omg is this a drinking game…), and before we knew it, it was all over — time to go get breakfast.

We're all stuck in situations that we don't like sometimes. Sitting at the DMV. Stuck in your cubicle on a slow day at the office and you ran out of internet to scroll through. Whatever you might be trapped in today, think about how you would have handled the situation as a child. Look around your environment — is there anything you can make a silly game out of? I'm sure there is! Channel that little creative spark inside you and turn the mundane into the best game ever.

HAVE FUN

This one goes without a huge explanation. Seriously, just go have fun today. I don't care where you are, or what's on your plate today. Make the time to burn some mental/physical/spiritual energy out and HAVE SOME FUN.

How would you feel if a child came up to you and said that they didn't have any fun today? You'd probably be like wow, that's insanely sad. Well, it makes ME sad that you could potentially go through a fun-less day. Don't let your inner child down! Adults need fun too, probably even more so than children. Go get it.

FORGIVE WITHOUT GRUDGES

As an adult, we go through challenges with others that have the potential to wound us to the core. People betray us, let us down, and burn us on extremely personal levels. Sometimes you have to cut people out of your life in order to move forward, and that's OK and healthy. You work towards forgiving that person within your heart so that you can be at peace. But are you really at peace if you "forgive" that person but still harbor negative energy in the form of a grudge?

Is there still a small part of you that hopes the worst for the person that hurt you? Are you telling everyone that you forgave them and moved on but you secretly hope that they get what they deserve? If so, you haven't truly forgiven.

Think back to when you were a child and your best friend did something that really made you upset. Chances are, you either worked it out and forgot all about it, or you stopped being friends with that other child and eventually moved on without attachment. Channel this part of you today and think about someone you're still holding a grudge over. Set yourself free.

BUILD FRIENDSHIPS

My mom used to take me everywhere as a kid. And I LOVED it because I loved new people. I was so intrigued by them and wanted everyone to be my friend. I used to scream "HI" at people in the supermarket louder and louder and louder until I got a return hello. I couldn't make enough random friends.

Regardless of whether you're introverted or extroverted, chances are at one point in your life, you'd strike up a conversation with a stranger without thinking twice about it. You didn't care about how you'd be received, you just started talking. And sometimes, you'd walk away with a new relationship. You carried this amazing skill with you to school and the playground and before long, you had a circle of kick-ass tiny friends.

Have you let this part of you go? Are you set in your ways and closed off to new people, comfortable with your circle? Think back to the last time you had an interesting conversation with a stranger. Was it so long ago you can't even remember? Your challenge today is to talk to someone you don't know and see what happens. It could be as simple as a quick chat in line on your way to grab coffee this morning.

The world moves forward when people connect with each other. A small random connection you make today could turn into something magical down the road. Are you open to finding out?

ADAPT TO CHANGE

I was at the nail salon recently talking to my manicurist and she was telling me about how excited her kids were to get back to school this coming year because they love to learn. And then she told me that she couldn't believe their enthusiasm because she was sending them both to a new school. She keeps waiting for them to start getting nervous, but then she realized that she was the only nervous one! Her kids couldn't wait to experience something new, even if that something was going to completely change and shape their world. And how funny is it that the parents are the ones freaking out over such a change.

Change is uncomfortable. It pushes us out of that comfy space of familiarity but it also pushes us into new levels of potential. No one's ever gone on to do great things by consistently staying in the same place.

Where in your life are you resisting change? What would happen if you approached it with excitement and enthusiasm instead of dread? Today, I challenge you to find out.

LAUGH

I made a conscious decision about ten years ago to stop censoring myself when I think something is funny, no matter how inappropriate it might be. There's nothing worse than stifling a genuine laugh — it NEEDS to come out!

When you were a child, you laughed at whatever was funny, and you laughed HARD. There is something so contagious about a kid cracking up at something, even if you have no idea what it is. The same goes for adults.

We've been conditioned to be more and more serious as we got older, and for what? To fit into a serious world? I don't know about you, but the last time I checked, the world is really anything but serious. Find something today that really makes you laugh and laugh about it unapologetically. Maybe you replay a YouTube video that makes you literally DIE and show your coworkers. Even if they don't find it funny, they will most certainly LOL by proxy. Get your giggles on!

EXPLORE

One day, I found an old key on the top of a door frame above my parents' bedroom. It was the coolest looking key I've ever seen, like an old-timey key from a fantasy movie. I was convinced that there was a secret door within a wall of my house that was covered over. I spent the day tapping every single wall of my house, trying to find a hollow hidden portal, and I'm pretty sure I enlisted my sister as an assistant. My mom thought we were nuts but she let me tap around anyway.

Turns out the key was to the original doorknobs that came with the house, which were very old-timey. No secret portals found but it was still awesome getting to explore the possibility!

Set aside some time today to explore something you're curious about. Maybe take a different street on your way to lunch today, or watch a documentary about something that really makes you wonder. The inner you is dying to explore something — feed your inner Sherlock Holmes.

EXPERIMENT

Every child gets to a point in their lives where they're given the authority to dress themselves. There comes a day when whoever usually dresses them says "OK, today you're going to choose your outfit." And what comes after that is usually a straight-up free comedy show. Some kids crossdress. Some kids pick out the most random combinations of colors and patterns. My sister had a period of her little life where she refused to wear anything without a Disney princess on it. I went through a phase in middle school where I wouldn't wear anything that didn't channel a 60s flower child or a 70s disco hall, sometimes putting the two together. We all look back on these photos of us and cringe but what was actually happening was amazing. We were refining our own style! You experimented until you eventually settled into some kind of algorithm that was uniquely YOU. And you'll probably keep refining this as you continue to grow and change and become more and more yourself. Because we never fully stop.

Where in your life could you experiment? Is there something about you that feels like a stagnant puddle? Maybe you haven't picked up a new hobby in a while. Maybe you're sick of eating the same old planned meals over and over. And maybe your wardrobe needs a refresh! Spend a little time today experimenting with new things that interest you. Chances are you'll find the room for something new.

BE A SUPERHERO

Growing up, I admired the courage of every single Disney princess. They were MY superheroes. They overcame challenges and stood their ground, but the most amazing quality that I saw in them was that they stuck up for their people. Belle stuck up for her cray cray father when he was trying to show the world his wild inventions. Pocahontas stuck up for her people when the new world was trying to take over her land. Jasmine stuck up for Aladdin because she knew that true love transcended the boundaries of social class.

I took this to heart at a very early age and vowed to always stand up for what I believed in. Through the years, I admittedly lost this ability and it's taken me a long time to realize that the person I needed to stick up for the most was myself. But all I have to do when in doubt is ask "What Would a Disney Princess Do?" WWDPD and I'm brought right back.

Who was your superhero growing up? Who did you admire and what qualities did you emulate in them? Spend some time today reflecting on that and bring those qualities into your life in some way today.

ASK FOR WHAT YOU WANT

As a child, you didn't think twice about asking for what you needed. Snacks. Answers. Reasons why. Potty breaks. You asked for it all and expected it all.

As adults, we feel weak when we have to ask for things. When we can't do it all ourselves, we hesitate to admit that we need other people and wind up struggling through situations that would be so much easier had we reached out with a simple request for a helping hand.

We are innately born with a need to connect and help our fellow humans, and we are also innately born to utilize that help when we need it. Think about a situation that you have been putting off asking for help with, even though you know it's needed. Make even a small step today towards reaching out. Identify that person and make the commitment to reach out.

I used to spend a lot of time at the local library as a child and was lucky enough to have an amazing aunt who ran things. One day, I discovered this book series where the main character of each story had some sort of god-given "obstacle" to overcome. There was a girl who was born with AIDS. A blind girl. A child that stuttered. Someone with diabetes. I was fascinated and so intrigued with these characters and read every single book. I couldn't believe how amazing these kids were — they took marginalized disabilities and turned them into superpowers. WOW!

When you see someone with any of these characteristics today, how do you react? Does a part of you cringe in secondhand embarrassment? Do you pretend like you don't see them at all? What would happen if you looked at someone who makes you feel a bit uncomfortable because you feel sorry for what they lack and decided to look at them as a person with secret super abilities? As crazy as it may seem, you could gain so many valuable realizations that you never thought possible. Keep this in mind as you journey through the day. Let's look at our differences with wonder and awe, whatever they may be.

DREAM BIG

"When I grow up, I want to be an artist." I wrote this on several "when I grow up" exercises and always envisioned myself drawing, painting, writing amazing things for a living. I dreamed of being a creator.

The world I grew up in sent me strong messages that this kind of life would be hard for me. Too hard and too painful because I wouldn't be able to make a living off of just "creating" stuff. So I took a different path. I studied and pushed and worked my way through careers that made me feel like an impostor. And for several years, I couldn't figure out why this was the case. Was I not confident enough? Is there something wrong with me?

When I got back in touch with my inner child and started to connect with successful, creative people who were thriving and living their best lives doing what they were best AT, the little artist in me started to wake up. My big dreams of living my life as a creator were reborn, and almost overnight, the concept of the Inner Child Project was born as well!

What big dreams of yours have you let go of? Is the little kid inside of you tugging at you to remember what you always wanted to do with your life? Dream big today.

APPRECIATE THE LITTLE THINGS

Right outside of my office, I am watching a building being built a couple of blocks over. These people are uber amazing, they literally build a floor of this place EVERY SINGLE DAY! I've watched the crane get higher and higher. I've watched it take carts of men up and down the side of the building. I've watched port o' potties hoisted up higher and higher so that the workers on the top floor aren't left stranded (by far my favorite observation).

I realized one day as I looked out that I could really do a better job of appreciating life's little wonders like this. Humans are literally building a high-rise building right before my eyes and that's pretty effing awesome. Just as my nephew gets a huge kick out of watching airplanes take off and land at the airport, I've tapped into that same sense of wonder and awe.

And so can you — the world is constantly offering us infinite chances to appreciate just how amazing life can be. Take a moment today to notice something seemingly ordinary and realize just how incredible it is.

LET YOURSELF NEED PEOPLE

You couldn't have made it to where you are today unless you needed people. Literally, before you were born, you were completely dependent on your mother to get you through to your birth date. And after that, you needed a whole village of people to raise you and help you grow into a successful adult. Never once did you think twice about it or feel like you were being too needy, too helpless. You simply received the help and it in turn helped you grow. When we grow up, we come into our own and learn to be independent in many ways, but that still doesn't eliminate our need for the help of others. We can't do everything ourselves. We all have within us a unique set of skills and natural abilities, and we also lack those that we can find in others. It's like a giant, mystical, amazing puzzle.

What are you struggling with today that you could reach out to others for help with? Have you been telling yourself that you don't need help because you are strong enough to handle it alone? If you were, you wouldn't be struggling. Think about your network and make it a point to reach out to someone today. If you're not grappling with an issue, use today to take a mental inventory of all those in your life you can lean on in times of trouble. Honor your tribe and send them love.

INVENT SOLUTIONS

There's an infamous story about me as a toddler breaking out of my playpen. My mom dropped me in and went upstairs to take care of something, and she turned around and there I was all of a sudden, climbing up the stairs. She had a total WTF moment. Upon an initial inspection, she couldn't figure out how I climbed out without knocking the whole thing over. And then she realized that I didn't climb out — I pulled the floor up from underneath and weaseled my way out the bottom. Talk about resourceful! I figured out the equivalent of a semi-complex math problem before I could even speak. Genius in the making.

Chances are you know of a similar story, whether it's with your own children, children you know, or even your own memories from childhood. Are you underestimating your ability to come up with solutions to problems you're close to giving up on? As we get older, this mental ability has the tendency to get clouded over in self-doubt and insecurity. Today, I challenge you to dust off the murk and recharge the batteries of your kid-powered genius. You have all of the answers you need, even if it takes you a bit longer to process the solution.

MOVE FORWARD

When your team lost a game in a sport you played as a kid, did you stop playing in future games? If you fell off your bike when the training wheels came off, did you stop trying to ride? When you missed a couple of notes in the song you had to play, did you stop going to band practice? Chances are you didn't. You pressed on and figured out how to get through it. You didn't give up. But maybe you DID give up. Maybe you realized that you hated the clarinet. Maybe you finally were like, "you know what, mom? Don't sign me up for soccer next year." And then you chose something else to focus on. Something that better suited you.

Either way, **YOU MOVED FORWARD**. You didn't let some slip up paralyze you from further action. You simply filed the experience away as a learning opportunity and pressed on. So often, we adults get so caught up in the ego's aversion to failure that we just give up, or worse — we don't even try at all.

What would you tell a child if they came to you and said they wanted to just stop trying? Say these same things to yourself when you're thinking about giving up. You were born to move forward, born to take on the world.

FORGET ABOUT SELF IMAGE

When I was a little girl, when I looked in the mirror, I saw magic. I saw superpowers and rainbows and all of my potential. I saw a strong, funny, outspoken little me, ready to take on the world. Sometimes I'd look in the mirror and make a funny face at what was staring back at me, but only if something looked a bit off. And by off, I mean it was a day where mom wasn't around and dad did my ponytail (seriously, just not the same). But I hardly let that stop me from conquering whatever adventure faced me that day.

Fast forward to my early teens and twenties and everything drastically changed. I was pelted with society's polluted messages that what I saw in the mirror was no longer acceptable. Cue decades of my working through so many issues stemming from this that I lost count.

Wherever you are on your journey of coming to terms with your own unique and fabulous body, your vow today is to look at yourself the way you did when you were a child.

Whenever you hold a child up to a mirror and say "who's that?", 99% of the time, they beam and give you a resounding, confident, proud AF "THAT'S ME!!!!" Today, look in the mirror with that same mindset. You are magically perfect.

EMBRACE LIFE'S CRAZINESS

About a month ago, I decided it was time for me to really get smart about my financial situation. I worked up a whole new budget plan and cancelled a ton of subscriptions to things that I had completely forgotten about (freeing up over a hundred bucks a month!!!). I resurrected an online budget tracker and analyzed my bank statements inside and out. I felt amazing and in control.

And then the next day, I checked my bank account and in ONE withdrawal, someone stole over 1400 dollars from me. Just like that — poof, gone. Instead of spending that day basking in my new budget freedom, I spent most of it at the bank trying to sort out the fraud, close my old accounts, open new ones, redo my online banking stuff...the whole thing.

I could have chosen to wallow in self-pity and convince myself that the universe would conspire against me, but I chose to laugh. I mean, how genuinely absurd is that whole situation?!?! Super freakin' hilarious. Life basically wrote me a sitcom that day.

Life is truly absurd and no one appreciates this more than kids. While my situation isn't something a kid would find hilarious, the lesson is still the same. When life hands you absurdity, the appropriate response is to laugh and then learn. I made some funny Instagram posts out of the whole thing and then took this as a hint from the universe that I should keep making financial responsibility a commitment no matter what. Is there anything in your life that you can reframe into a laughable lesson? LOL at life today, no matter how many unfunny things it throws.

ASK QUESTIONS

Why is the sky blue? Why is the grass green? Where do babies come from?

Kids are constantly asking questions about anything and everything. That's how they start shaping their worldview!

They ask about everything from the mundane to the impossible to answer. They want to know why the dog walks on four legs but we walk on two. They want to know why it gets dark at night. They want to know why we have to put gas in the car.

At some point in our lives, we transition from asking about everything to learning how to just accept things for what they are. And sometimes, this is valuable. But other times, it's detrimental. When we stop questioning things at a fundamental level, we stop growing. We stop wanting to change things we don't agree with. We get scared of finding out that the answer to an unasked question might damage us in some way. So we just stop asking.

What questions do you have burning inside but have been afraid to ask? Is there something you know you need the answer to? Today, Google that question. Or ask a friend or coworker. Channel that inner child that needs to know anything and everything and won't let up until they get an answer.

MOVE THROUGH YOUR FEELINGS

I watched an Instagram story of someone I follow of their baby smiling and laughing, and then all of a sudden they started hysterically crying out of nowhere. What the hell happened?! I'm sure we've all witnessed little kid temper tantrums where they go from zero to 238742084 in less than a minute, and then after they calm down, it's like nothing ever happened.

What do we do when kids are super emotional? We let them "cry it out". We let them fully express themselves until they've felt all the feels, and then they come back to reality. And they come back every single time. It's just a part of life.

Something happens when we're adults and we start suppressing our emotions because they're immature. They aren't manly. They signify you not holding your shit together. They tell people you're weak.

While throwing yourself on the floor in the middle of the breakroom at work because your boss is the biggest D-Bag ever is probably inappropriate, going into the bathroom or taking a walk to really let yourself feel your emotions is perfectly fine. You need to let these things out. You need to honor what comes up so you can process and learn from it. Just like with kids, you need to let yourself cry it out sometimes. Honor your emotions today — the good, the bad, and the unpopular ugly.

BE UNAPOLOGETICALLY YOU

I laugh at things that would make other people cringe. I have a notorious potty mouth. I can't wear high heels without wanting to die. I cry pure tears of joy every time I hear Enigma's "Return to Innocence". I'm extremely stubborn. I am late to whatever I'm not excited about going to. I procrastinate. I'm extremely passionate about conspiracy theories (which are of course all 100% true facts). I named my dog after a philosopher. I am a clairsentient/claircognizant empathic psychic.

And after many, many years of trying to be everything I'm not, I can now type out these insanely amazing traits above and beam with pride. This is who I am. This is who I was always meant to be. As Kid Cudi says, "I'm just what you made, God."

We come into this world as infinitely unique, gifted souls, each with a unique set of skills and flaws that come together so beautifully. And we know this at a very very early age. It's not until society pushes us all into molds we don't belong in that we lose our way. And it can take what feels like a lifetime to undo.

No matter how far you've strayed from who you really are, today I want you to take just one quality about yourself that you try to hide from the world, but are secretly proud of. What would it feel like to bring that out of the closet today? Are you willing to try?

KNOW YOU ARE FREE

Go back to a moment in your life where you were a child and completely lost track of time. Where you were caught up in absolute bliss, just lost in the experience. Maybe you were at an amusement park with your cousins and in what felt like a blink, the day was over. Maybe you were lost in a computer game, fully immersed from noon to night solving mysteries, until you realized it was time to go to bed. Or maybe you got so wrapped up in the magic of the ocean and sand on the beach one day, that before you knew it, the sun was setting.

In moments like this, you experienced what it was like to be truly free. Free from the concept of time. Free from constraints of everyday life stopping you from feeling the flow of the universe that everyone craves as an adult.

But the funny thing is, we can still have these moments, and we don't have to go as far as planning a vacation to an ultra-remote part of the world to remember what it feels like.

What makes you feel free? What could help you get totally lost for a while that's just within your reach? Really think about this today and commit to finding it. You are free by nature. All you have to do is let go.

BE GENEROUS

It feels good to give to others without attachment. It's one of life's mysteries that we take for granted. Giving to someone without a second thought almost creates the same kind of buzz you get when you take that first sip of coffee or tea in the morning. It taps into that same part of you that is overcome with joy at the sight of something awe-inspiring in nature. It hits the same nerve as when you accomplish a goal you've been working on for what feels like forever.

We teach children that sharing is caring, and it's pretty much a life covenant. Teaching a young child to share can be difficult at times and it's also hilarious. I think about my sister teaching my nephew to share things with my niece and laugh because it seems like such a simple concept. But think about your own life today. Are you really sharing all that you need to share, or are you hoarding toys?

And sharing doesn't necessarily have to mean material things. Are you hanging on to ideas that really need to be let go in the world to make it a better place? Are you afraid that if you share, something will be taken away from you or stolen? Your challenge today is to get creatively generous, whatever that might mean to you.

UNBOUND IMAGINATION

I used to have this game when I was a kid that was so awesome. It was basically this box filled with a couple of random props (plastic crystals, cards, some other little trinkets) and a cassette tape. To play the game, you popped in the cassette tape and this fairy godmother spoke from the other side and painted a five-minute scenario with an action step at the end. What followed were hours and hours of just the best, most imaginative play, EVER. We literally created a whole new reality for hours and hours and it felt like we were somewhere else.

We got to be magical beings on planet earth, solving mysteries and searching for lost secrets. It was such an amazing experience. I wonder whatever happened to that game by the way…if anyone out there knows about this game PLEASE let me know!!

The more I get back in touch with my life's purpose and trust in the guidance of the universe, the more I'm realizing that we really do create our own realities. While we probably can't choose to turn into a fairy for the rest of our lives, we DO have the power to choose happiness. To imagine a life beyond our wildest dreams and keep imagining it until it really does start to become a reality.

This kind of trust and mindset doesn't come easily and surely not overnight, but your capacity for an unbound imagination is alive and well deep within you. Today, take a moment to get quiet and really imagine yourself living the life of your dreams. What comes up for you? Can you take away one small step from your imagination that will help you make those dreams a reality?

CONNECT

I took a yoga class over the weekend right before I wrote this and what happened was such a beautiful microcosm of how important it is to connect and how we tend to view it in today's world. I got my groggy Saturday morning self over to the studio and took a nice quiet place in the back and got comfortable on my mat. I really wanted some quiet and was lying down, taking in the soft music and relishing in the time I had to myself. All of a sudden, the teacher walked in and abruptly made everyone stand up. She told us to look around the room and start talking to someone you didn't know. And I noticed my first reaction was one of annoyance. I'm just here for yoga and to center myself, screw everyone else today.

But I looked at the women around me and, almost instantly, my heart was warmed by their openness to the invitation to connect with me, whether they really wanted to on the inside or not. And in our brief exchange, I got to meet three like-minded women who were all waking up early on a Saturday for the same reasons as me.

I know I mentioned this already, but I can't express to you how important it is to keep our connections with the world open and strong. As children, this came so easily to us. Yet, as we get older, we slowly withdraw and our circles become smaller and smaller. We get annoyed with others, tuning out different viewpoints, styles, and life choices. We get uber judgmental.

I am choosing to challenge you to connect on this last day of the journey because it's truly what keeps you alive. Today, share what you learned over the last month with someone who needs it. Who do you know that could really use a nudge to get back in touch with their innate gifts and abilities? Look how far you've come and share that with another person.

You were born to do amazing things and you are an amazing human being. You are a childlike, free spirit who is having a perfectly, messy, confusing, intense, beautiful human experience. You never lost your inner child, they are always with you. They are always just a smile away.

* * *

how are you feeling? childish AF? inspired to color on some walls? craving chicken nuggets and mac & cheese? i know i am. i always am.

stay connected to the little bugger that lives inside your

soul. they know more about us than we do. as long as you guys are a team, your inner compass will be on straight, trust me. return to your innocence whenever you feel yourself flying off the "adulting is way too much" handle. because it IS too much to handle.

adulthood is absurd, way too serious, and extremely overrated. just ask any (inner) child.

losing my religion

that's me in the corner.

or it kinda felt more like a spotlight half the time, because thinking what i thought and feeling what i felt as a kid growing up catholic made me feel like i stood out. except i didn't stand out because no one really knew what i was thinking or feeling except for me. i never told anyone, never really outwardly questioned it, never had any conversations about it until i was much, much older.

and even after you could say that i "left" the catholic church, there was no drama. it just…was. it just happened. and i think that's why i loved the process so much. it was the most elegant, eloquent, come to jesus (pun intended) meeting with my higher self over my entire life that resulted in me having the most incredible personal relationship with my creator.

i'd come across people here and there, through dating and college, friendships, philosophy classes — other people who had grown up in a pretty hard-core religious environment who didn't quite buy it. some were more loudly opposed than others. but i felt a deep connection with all of them. and with the exception of a small few, no one was really proud of abandoning their childhood religion. it's not exactly something you shout from the rooftops. it's not really something to brag about, i don't think.

maybe because when you tell people you're "not religious", they assume you're an atheist. or you're a satan worshipper. and if they're assuming that, then there's really no point in trying to explain your views to them. it's not something some people can grasp. and that's OK. they're not who i'm talking to.

i'm talking to anyone who's wrestled with their inherited religious belief system. anyone who knows what it's like to feel that deep pit in your stomach that something just isn't jiving and you're not really sure why. the people who silently make their way through a religious life with a secret — the secret of knowing their own relationship with god (or whatever you call it/him/her).

i talk to god all the time. we're besties. and god comes to me in many different shapes and sizes, colors, patterns, voices. we are amazingly close. i never leave home without this connection. i've always had it. and as i walked through my life, seemingly losing my religion since birth, i've been held so closely the entire fucking time.

my relationship with catholicism is a complicated, beautiful mess of a mental dilemma. and i love it so much because i think it might have been the easiest part of my awakening, ironically.

but i know that for many people, it's not so easy. leaving a religion oftentimes is an extremely difficult choice, filled with loneliness, misunderstanding, shunning, and an assortment of other alienating shit feelings and consequences. it's a personal decision and the steps leading up to it are all so incredibly unique. there's no way that any one person could tell another how to go about dismantling their pre-set radio station that is a religious belief system. you just can't go there.

but what you can do is share stories of how YOU did it. which is exactly what i'm about to do. let's start from the beginning.

* * *

i was born on april 25th, 1985, to two loving parents. they're both catholic and came from catholic families (with the exception of my paternal grandfather who was protestant, which i feel like everyone always forgets). i was baptized shortly after i was born — i could text my mom right now and ask her for the date but it's not THAT important. just know that i came into this world amongst many catholics and was thrown right in.

i went to church every sunday with my family. my sister was born in '88 and once she came along, she did church too. live from the baby carrier. all of us sitting in the wooden pew, sometimes going into this sectioned-off area known as the "cry room", which was literally for loud-ass kids. my mom used to make jokes that it was where the bad kids went. there was this plexiglass partition that you could look through from the main part of the church, so you could spy on these bad apples like they were zoo animals. pretty entertaining once you ran out of goldfish crackers and coloring book pages to kill the time. anyway...

i never really liked church that much. i never really understood why we were there, and even when i got to school, things didn't clear up for me. my dad would always say things like "it's a sacrifice you make" and i would always think, "for what?" i mean what the hell were we sacrificing? some extra hours of sleep? what if we were exhausted and needed to sleep to feel better? wouldn't god want us to feel better? and isn't he EVERYWHERE anyway? i mean, couldn't you just like...pray from your bed? whatever.

my parents sent me to catholic school, starting with kindergarten. i went to the same school through eighth grade. the parish we belonged to and the church we went to had a school that was essentially attached. we lived about eight blocks away and most of my neighbors went to the same school with me. we'd carpool most mornings and then when we got old enough, we'd walk home. i remember my one neighbor's mom would always play michael bolton.

i had to wear a uniform. it was a blue and white plaid jumper from first grade to fifth grade, and then, in sixth grade, you could wear a gray skirt and a blouse. everyone was so jazzed about the skirts because they signified you were older, wiser. and you could roll them up and show some fucking LEG! but by the time i got to skirt age, we had a new principal who was a straight-up tyrant.

one day, she stopped me in the hallway and asked me if my skirt was rolled. it was, and she knew it — not sure why she fucking asked me but authority figures love asking you rhetorical questions. she sent me to the office downstairs where they had this nun outfit (a habit, they're called) hanging up that she was going to make me change into and wear for the rest of the day, as a punishment for rolling up my skirt.

no fucking WAY i was doing that, how humiliating! i balled my eyes out and asked to call my mom. my mom asked to talk to the secretary and eventually i got out of it. and i thought to myself, how the fuck is this christ-like at all? does god really care about what i'm wearing? does he care that maybe i feel a little bit nicer if i roll my skirt up a little bit? i mean, i'm not even trying to get any attention from boys, i'm just trying to not feel like a fucking NUN. wouldn't god want me to feel great? and why are we all wearing the same outfits anyway? what's the point of that? i thought god loved all of his children and made us all unique individuals.

we also had religion books, which honestly (and i'm sorry to have to put it this way) were pretty much propaganda. i wish i would have saved some of them because they were pretty intense. i do remember some of what was in there though. like i remember one year there was a small section on "the occult" and, of course, i was so drawn to it. everyone was. i remember my teacher pointing out the picture of the ouija board and telling us that it was devil worship. meanwhile, i had several friends who had these boards and i didn't think they were satan worshippers. and when we played with it, we never summoned the devil. i think one time someone's ouija board told someone they were going to die, and that never happened either.

i also remember a religion book revealing to me that santa wasn't real. there was this page of pictures and we had to circle what was real and what wasn't and there was an elf picture. i was in like third grade and no one had popped my santa cherry yet so i didn't circle it, and neither did most of my classmates. when it came time for us to check the answers, my teacher told us that HER teacher book didn't have the elf circled and we were all like umm WHY? and then i think when she realized what happened, she backtracked and told us that elves were real. but fuck that, the damage was already done for me. i went home and spanish inquisitioned my parents for weeks until they finally caved and told me the truth, and told me not to tell my sister. but i wound up telling her like within a year. while we were watching "the santa clause" starring tim allen, in the back room at my grandparents' house.

the more i went through school and the more it was drilled into my head that god loves everyone unconditionally, the more i realized that what i was learning and the rules being imposed on me were the complete opposite of what i thought a loving god and jesus would want for me. and i understood this at a very early age. and honestly, i never felt bad about it.

i heard about someone in the parish getting pregnant — an older girl, in high school — and i found out she wasn't allowed in church anymore. i mean, how come? wouldn't a person going through something so scary need all the god they could get? why was she not allowed to come? i didn't understand.

i also really never understood the sacraments either. especially penance, or confession. first of all, i am not sure why they make an eight-year-old confess their sins. what sins does a fucking eight year old have? i remember so vividly racking my little brain over what bad things i did so i had something to tell the priest. i told him i talked back to my mom and i said some bad words. and he was so kind and sweet and he explained to me that my little kid sins were forgiven. i felt great! i ran out of there like i was some kind of clean little super soul.

and then the inevitable happened — i talked back to my mom again. this sent me into a spiral. i'm not clean anymore! i have to go back to confession! how fast can i get there? but wait a minute…

eight-year-old me was like, isn't this kind of pointless? i'm ultimately going to screw up my entire life, over and over again. i watch all the adults in my life do it, why would i be any different? god HAS to know this, right? i mean, he made us after all. and in his image, right? and why do i need to tell another human being about all of the human being screw-ups that i involve myself in? if the priest is human, doesn't he fuck up too? who does HE talk to?

it just didn't make sense to me then. but i still went to confession after that because we had to in catholic school. i remember getting yelled at in the dark little confessional once when i was a bit older for forgetting the words to this one prayer we had to say before talking about our fuck ups. the priest actually gave me extra prayers to say on top of the regular punishment ones. like what the hell was up with that?

i threw in the towel completely on confession in high school, when confession became optional. they'd sit us all in the auditorium, spaced out a few seats all around each person, you know, to give us space to think about how much we've all been fucking up. they even gave us these menu-looking laminated pamphlets that outlined each of the ten commandments with everything you could possibly do to violate them in a neat, catholic guilt-tripping bulleted format.

no thanks, never again. am i going to hell? maybe. but i simply couldn't have cared less. making that decision to never have to tell my "sins" to an old man again was the first of my religious freedom stakes in the ground. the first of many.

* * *

things that i questioned early on in my childhood continued to challenge me until i eventually realized my higher self was guiding me through formulating my own unique relationship with god. and i trusted this guidance so deeply, you could say it was really the first time i whole-heartedly trusted my intuition.

it lead me to a deeply personal, deeply loving relationship with god. MY god, MY creator. not the picture of god painted for me by an institution that is so far from perfect. what i questioned in my inherited religion ultimately paved the way for me to become a deeply spiritual person. and paved the way for me to keep trusting the nudges from spirit that held my hand through my awakening.

i have a lot of catholics in my family, who i respect and love dearly. they are amazing people. i am happy that they live a faith that makes them happy and i am glad that they can connect with god in a way that i hope is as personal as my connection. there was never really a time when i stood up and...announced my departure. because i don't think it was needed. i'm not angry about it. i'm not trying to make a stink, or try to convince anyone that i'm right/they're wrong. how could i know?

the only thing i know for sure is that cultivating a deeply personalized relationship to god/source/creator/whatever you'd like to call it is so crucial to awakening — at least it was for me. the journey can be lonely and daunting. you'll feel so misunderstood. you're reinventing yourself and that breaking out of the cocoon is so so painful. you need someone to hold you through it.

and that's what MY god does. we're never apart. my god laughs with me when it's all just too much to bear. cries with me when i don't know what else to do. and because i trust god so much, i know i'll always be OK, no matter what. i wouldn't trade this relationship for anything.

if you're struggling with breaking up with a religion, have faith that there's nothing wrong with you. you're no heathen. if you're feeling a pull to explore your own belief system and relationship to source, know that those pulls are coming from source itself. because the universe wants you to have a deeply personal, authentically tailored love affair with it.

and you'll know once you find it. you'll know because your questioning will get replaced with a deep, graceful peace. you are so incredibly loved, at the absolute highest levels, because you ARE those highest levels. you are an expression of god and, therefore, you are the most precious, special gift that ever was. you can only realize this through a whole lot of trust and connection with your heart.

keep going. keep trusting. have faith that you are so loved. you always were and always will be. always.

authenticity*

authenticity isn't free.
it cost me my career.
it cost me friendships.
it cost me the security that is
being someone that everyone else
wanted me to be.

it forced me to shed
parts of me that people loved.
and it forces me to wake up
every single morning with
the question of:
"how can i really be ME today?"

and it hurts.
it burns.
it's confusing.
it breaks me down.

it's the hard work most people don't want to do.
it's the nag inside of me that got
so loud i couldn't push it down anymore.
it's the force that drives me.
it's what keeps me sane.
it is my inner compass.

authenticity is a journey,
but it is also home.

so be you,
no matter what it costs you.
that is why you're here
on this planet.

it really is that simple.

criminal

i half-jokingly, half-seriously, would tell my friends that i'd eventually write a book about my dating escapades. about all of the assholes who took me for a ride. about all of the absolute dickbags who treated me like trash. about all of the weirdos i met online who were cool up until we met in person.

i had a rough outline put together. it was called "tales from the toolshed".

because it was always everyone else's fault why i couldn't hold down a relationship. it was always "something in the water". it was a new undiagnosed mental disease, plaguing the men of my generation. it was because i was too educated and such a catch that i intimidated most guys. it was because the bachelor lifestyle evolved into something unprecedented and no one would give it up.

it was a universal problem, not a "me" problem.

and it also couldn't explain why good people were getting into relationships around me, staying in them, and *GASP* getting married.

but no, the problem wasn't me. these girls nabbing great guys just got lucky. or these couples were just two idiots, staying together not because they really loved each other, but to keep up appearances. everyone was just doing it for their families. doing it for the social norms. doing it for the 'gram.

the book was called "tales from the toolshed" because everyone that i dated was a tool. a douchebag. a player. brain dead. a coward. immature. couldn't handle it. wasn't a man.

but here's the twist: i was a fucking tool too.

and i really couldn't admit it until now. because the karmic loop is closed and i can now look back and see what the hell was really going on.

so let's define a karmic loop for those of us new here:

Karmic loops are behaviors, emotions, thought-forms or dynamics that are repetitive in your life. When you are caught up in a karmic loop no matter what you try to do to change you always end up in the same place/state, but each time the karmic loop gets triggered, the emotional charge from that karmic loop becomes heavier and more troublesome. (from www.in-light-ment.com)

and you'll keep getting into the same tango of whatever it is until you crack the code. until you figure out what the lesson is. you can't transcend ANY problem in your life unless you get so stuck in it that you have no choice but to change.

believe me when i tell you that if you're really meant to learn something in this lifetime, it will be very evident what you'll need to do to transcend it. so evident, that it will be right in front of your face. it will be uncomfortable. it will make you feel like a dog turd on a hot sidewalk.

it will also make you want to run in the other direction, pretending that you don't see it. huge mistake, but it's what we tend to do.

but because the universe is SO fucking kind and really roots for us, even from the cheap seats, it will smack you in the face if you choose not to see. and the smack will hurt. you will bleed. you will drown. you will shit yourself.

and then you will change. you'll have no choice.

there is one way to avoid such hefty karmic bitch slaps: fine-tune that intuition of yours. you'll get hints every single day, but if you don't have the decoder, they'll fly right on by. unfortunately, you can't fine-tune that sucker until you get slapped a LITTLE bit. so my wish for you is that your slaps be ever in your favor. and that they don't kill you before you have a chance to learn.

* * *

it wasn't until i met my husband that i decided i wasn't going to be a tool anymore. it was an unconscious decision, but one that was made. when i met him, i just knew i was going to marry him. i just knew it was game over. can't explain how i was so sure, but i also can't explain how i can predict world happenings and read minds — it falls into that category of multidimensional magic.

i fell for him hard, almost immediately. and that feeling wasn't new. i'd experienced this phenomenon a zillion times. i rarely dated anyone i didn't fall for immediately. the difference this time was that i SAW the future.

this was the real deal.

so you can imagine how devastated i was that he dumped me out of the blue.

we had been dating for about four months when it happened. we'd met each other's families. i was just shy of planning our wedding. i was feeling that something was off in the weeks leading up to the breakup, but i had no idea that he was about to leave me.

it was the most giant karmic smack of my entire life.

* * *

up until this point, it was ME who had the upper hand in ending relationships. it was MY move to end something so the other person couldn't. it was MY superpower of avoiding intimacy. and it ripped many hearts from many men.

now don't get me wrong, a lot of these men i dated deserved getting a little bit of a smack from me. although i was somewhat of a runaway bride, i wasn't exactly the best at holding boundaries. i'd attract some really narcissistic type behavior into my life because i think it served as a counter-balance to my overly empathetic savior complex. everyone could be fixed in my eyes.

there's a line in springsteen's "human touch" about how he just needs a little touch-up paint job and he'll look a lot better. and it always makes me laugh because i feel like that was how i chose people. it was like my world was a flea market and i was looking for the flip of a lifetime. looking for beat-up fucking furniture i could re-do and invite everyone over to see the renovations and bask in the glow of everyone being impressed.

it wasn't their fault half the time. if i grew up in the environments i know most of them did, i'd turn out fucked up too. shit, i turned out fucked up and i really have no excuse. but we're all a little fucked up, aren't we?

they didn't deserve me to bolt without a warning. they deserved basic human respect. an adult conversation about why i wanted to end things.

but i just couldn't handle that kind of confrontation. i had enough of a hard time realizing i was so afraid of anyone getting close to me, let alone dealing with the lash out that would be me trying to have a breakup conversation with someone who was already a little bit volatile. it pained me so much to see another human being upset. and it was enough for me to simply know i was the cause. i couldn't pile on the actual physical drama that resulted from an honest breakup onto that guilt. so i just avoided it.

i left guys in the dust so many times, it would make your head spin. ripped the band-aid off relationships that everyone thought would last forever. but instead of telling everyone that hey, i think maybe i have an intimacy problem, it was easier to tell everyone that my new ex was a piece of shit tool bag.

and i'm really great at telling animated stories full of belly laugh-inducing humor, so i'm pretty sure i hooked my audience every single time. if they talked about how neurotic i must be behind closed doors, i didn't know it. it was too easy for me to avoid all of the necessary pains of human breakups through bypassing the entire thing and making sure everyone else has a great laugh on the way out.

sometimes i'd get back together with someone i'd completely trashed just weeks before. and then i'd craft some amazing, convincing story about how much they'd changed or pledged to change, and that all of that funny shit i'd told them was mostly an exaggeration. and please don't laugh at his deep dark secrets the next time you see him. or think about that embarrassing story that was supposed to be kept within the confines of our relationship that's now imprinted in your brain.

* * *

my husband broke up with me on june 17th, 2015. between 5 and 6pm. i had taken the day off from work to go have some medical testing done that would ultimately result in my gallbladder being removed. i was feeling like shit in general and was really looking forward to figuring out what was wrong with me. he had been acting weird the entire day, and i felt it. he was going to come over to my place for the weekend because my roommate at the time was away and we'd have the apartment to ourselves.

i had texted him to see what kind of food he wanted me to order for us and he replied that he wasn't hungry and to not worry about it. wtf, was he sick? maybe he was sick. now i was sick.

i remember taking a hit from the bowl of old weed i had (that was pretty much straight resin at this point) and blasting some loud techno music to calm myself down. it was nothing, it had to be nothing. maybe i still had the weird testing dye in my veins and it was making me mental. maybe i was PMSing.

he knocked on my door and i opened it. he was visibly upset. and then i looked down and he was holding some stuff. he was holding MY stuff. oh my god.

he came in and couldn't catch his breath. he handed me the pile of my clothes. the ones i had left at his place. and then he said it.

"i can't do this anymore."

i can feel the pain of those words all over again as i type. the most gut-wrenching internal split was taking place inside my body. i was hot. my insides were bursting apart at the seams. i could barely stand.

he said something about wanting to move to chicago, wanting to get away. me telling him i'd go with him wasn't the answer. maybe it was him. he needed time alone. he was sorry. he wanted to hug me. i didn't let him. he was crying, i was crying. then i yelled at him to leave.

he left.

i couldn't breathe. i couldn't move. and then i crumbled to the ground like a limp, dead mop.

i called my friends. i called my sister. they came over as soon as they could. they brought booze. i drank so much. we all talked for the rest of the night about what could have been the real reason, because i wasn't given one. i didn't know why he left. things were so good, i couldn't believe he left me.

i was assured it wasn't me. assured that i did nothing wrong. maybe he had a secret dark past. maybe he is a commitment-phobe. maybe he was fucked up like my other exes and i dodged a bullet. yep, that was it — i dodged a bullet. oh my god, could i IMAGINE what it would be like if we got married and he did this to me? what if we had kids? wow, i really am actually lucky he did this now and not down the road. ok, yeah — maybe this really worked out for the best.

i couldn't be alone that night so two of my best friends took me to their place. i was so drunk by then. we continued hashing everything over until was after midnight. i drank whiskey that night, and i hate whiskey. i have a picture still in my phone of this one fish in their fish tank that i slept next to on the couch that night. i remember falling asleep to his blank stare and finding a sort of comfort, feeling like things were going to be OK.

and then when i woke up, his dumb fucking fish stare reminded me that it WASN'T a nightmare. i was really single again and i wasn't in control of it. i re-lived the pain of the night before all over again. my friends took me to see a movie, i think it was an amy schumer movie. and they made me dinner that i could barely eat. and then i had to go home. and sleep alone.

but it would all be OK, right? because i'd be able to at least go to work on monday and get my head in the game and distract myself, you know? yeah, that would have worked. if my new ex didn't also work with me.

if you've ever dated someone you worked with and then it went sour, you know the level of awkwardness i'm talking about here. there's a saying about dating someone at work, "don't shit where you eat". and i completely fucking get it now. i don't wish this scenario on anyone.

i'd see him all the time. pass him in the hallways. he'd try to smile at me and i'd look the other way. or i'd occasionally fire the death stare of a lifetime directly in his eyes, that would ultimately wind up making ME feel like shit. probably more than he did. it sucked. massively.

and this went on for months. just when i thought i was going to have to quit to escape the absolute madness that is having to be in the same daily environment as someone who dumps you without a real reason, i started to get over it. i re-downloaded some dating apps. i got back in the game.

but none of these guys even compared. i just couldn't forget him. maybe it was too soon? i didn't know. all i knew was that i really didn't want to date anyone ever again.

and so i channeled my shitty feelings into doing things for me. i made it a point to do more things with friends, to go out more often instead of passing up opportunities. made a pact with my soul that i'd never get so wrapped up in a dude that i'd lose all of my friends. those days were over.

i threw myself into my job. i got into stand-up comedy. i had my gallbladder taken out in the name of self-care.

then in september he texted me. asked me if i wanted to get coffee or beers. what in the actual fuck.

what was THIS? why did he want to talk to me? did he want to apologize for leaving me so abruptly? did he want me back? did he want to return another item of clothing i'd left at his place that he found after moving some shit around his room? i didn't know.

i asked all of my friends what i should do. most of them told me to ignore it. don't talk to him. he's an asshole. and i don't even know why i asked them. because i knew he wasn't an asshole, not even close. and so i met up with him.

we met at a bar near my apartment. we got drunk as we fumbled through the initial awkwardness. you know what i mean. the kind where you bullshit about how great you're both doing. that weird flirting that is old and new at the same time. he told me he wanted another chance. he apologized to me. wanted to start over.

and of course i had my reservations. i played tough. but ultimately i told him i wanted to try again too. the timing was off when we first got together and now it was right. he was sure. and underneath my ego, i was sure too.

even though it took some time for me to trust that he wasn't going to leave me again. i eventually got over it. and not because i learned to trust that he wasn't going anywhere, it was more because i decided to surrender to the fact that some things were beyond my control. that people don't belong to other people. that you can't love another person truly until you commit to loving yourself. and note that i didn't say "until you learn to love yourself". i think that when you find the right person to love, the ability to love yourself fully and truly reveals itself to you over time. in the most perfect way.

it's obvious that this story has a happy ending. i've already referred to him as my husband. we've been happily married for about six months as i'm writing this. and we're so happy. because we're individuals, growing separately but together. we're truly best friends. through him, i learn something new about myself every single day. he is my mirror. he gives me the space to grow into the person i am meant to be, and i for him.

we're truly the best team.

and so the karmic loop has been closed. i don't have to run anymore because i've learned to stay when it's uncomfortable. i've learned to let someone love me even though it's risky, even though they could change their mind and leave me tomorrow, or drop dead. that's just the way life is. and if you're not taking risks in love, you're not living. you'll certainly die alone. safe, maybe — but alone.

* * *

to further close this chapter, i'd like to make a formal apology to everyone i've ever dated and hurt.

i'm sorry for all the times i left without an explanation. i'm sorry for sometimes running back and pretending i wanted you when, in reality, i was just lonely, or drunk. or both.

i'm sorry for when i bashed you to my family and friends without a chance for you to defend yourself. and i'm sorry for embellishing shit in the name of comedy that served to make me feel less guilty for bulldozing you.

i'm sorry for making things out to be your fault when i left, when i had just as much of a part to play.

i'm sorry for pretending like i was happy for months after i knew i wanted out. i'm sorry for putting on such a show.

i'm sorry for throwing out crazy shit about myself to make you feel bad for me. to make you feel bad about calling me out on my bullshit. to cry wolf when i should have just been a grown-ass woman about it.

i'm sorry for leaving you and immediately cutting all ties as if you never existed. i'm sorry for any pain you went through trying to figure out what happened and why i left. i'm sorry for making you think it was all you. or trying to, anyway. it was definitely sometimes me. sometimes a little bit, and sometimes mostly me.

i'm sorry for being immature and not facing you like an adult. i'm sorry for not being honest with you.

may this apology find who it needs to and land softly.

may you find the love you deserve. may you find peace and happiness and joy in a human counterpart. may you grow old with someone who loves you unconditionally. may the love you find transform you into the best version of yourself you know you're meant to be. and may you find it in your heart to forgive me, the woman you probably wrote off as a heartless bitch. she was really lost.

but she's learning.

although you may think she's the criminal fiona apple sings about, she did her time.

and she's home.

take me home

at some point in your awakening, you'll encounter a state of being that i like to call the ultimate cosmic funk. it blows. and how you arrive at it goes a little something like this:

you have your initial awakening experience where you realize that wanting to leave your old life behind is actually OK. so then you get excited. you make changes like leaving a shitty relationship or your shitty job. you grow your hair out and dye it pink because, hey fuck it! i'm ME, baby! look at me go!

and then you're on this high. you're high off the hard fact that no one really cares more than YOU about who you choose to be. amazing! but then, who are you? you're not really sure. so you dig. and you go deeper. and deeper. fall further down the rabbit hole.

and you realize that not only are you way more than who you thought you were, you're way more than human. yeah, i said it. and i know you know what i mean.

you realize you're more than your body. you're not from around here. you're back here to learn and explore and grow. you're playing a game. your higher self is propped up in the ether on one of those video game chairs and is like "why isn't this fucker doing anything i'm telling it to do?"

so you're like…seeing this phenomenon. you know it's real because you just know. you feel it in your bones. but it's beyond your bones. you know your body here on earth is just a product of the craziest simulation of all time and you're literally here to just have experiences. and they're supposed to be fun.

except you're not having fun. i mean, what the hell? so i kinda hacked the game. i get it now. why am i not having fun?

so you kinda zone out. you realize your knowledge alone of who you are doesn't unlock your highest self. no amount of pleidian youtube videos or tarot card pulls or crystals in your underwear can help you with the **BIG** thing you need help with. integrating the awareness that you're so much **MORE** than this goes beyond just knowing about it.

and then you're like "well, **THAT** is just too high of a task and **WAY** too much to ask. i'm just going to completely tune out the world around me and act like i'm sitting on planet 923490-G because it's **SO** much nicer there. i'm **SO** much better than this stupid ass game. it hurts to live on this planet, and it stinks. no, literally, it really fucking smells in this city. ugh gross. get me out of here."

TAKE ME HOME.

because knowing your ultimate home is beyond the four walls of your condo/city/country/planet is the ultimate dick tease. who the fuck would want to be **HERE** when you can be **THERE**? except you really **CAN'T** be there because you're supposed to be HERE. but why even let me KNOW about THERE then?

this is the ultimate cosmic funk. it's fucking awful. if you've ever been there, i am both so proud of you and so sorry you're sitting in it. lord jesus, have mercy. and if you haven't been there yet or have just realized you're balls deep in it, i hope this chapter helps you through.

in the middle of my cosmic funk, i heard phil collins' "take me home". it made me turn into a puddle. it sounded like me trying to bargain with someone from THERE. get me the fuck OUTTA HERE. i'm tired of uncovering the hard truths about this place. this planet is literally a prison. i'm a slave to the system and i numb out any chance i can.

and um, excuse me but ALSO! i'm learning SO much about who i really am and all of my power and i'm getting past life glimpses etc. etc. but i can't FULLY REMEMBER? what kind of dumbass bargain is THAT? like don't you think it would give me a leg up if i had just a TINY amount of information? like if you just let me know for SURE that i was joan of arc, it would REALLY help my confidence in maybe helping humanity during a global civilization collapse.

TAKE ME HOME.

and then i remembered that my current interpretation was not my original. my parents were HUGE phil collins fans. so much so that we joked that he was our "uncle phil". he was always on. in the car, while mom was cleaning, down the jersey shore, out in the garage.

one of the best memories i have and am so grateful for is when i took my parents to a phil collins show. in my last company's luxury box seats. right after i put my two weeks in. an epic experience on multiple different levels.

my dad always told me that "take me home" reminded him of his dad, my grandfather. he was a prisoner of war during WWII. he was captured in the philippines and was transferred to several different prison camps for 3.5 years. "take me home" could have been about how he was able to survive, how he was able to come home, mind mostly intact, after enduring some of the most grueling physical and mental torture known to mankind.

he had no contact with the outside world. the japanese would come to his cell and tell him that they killed his entire family. read his home address back to him. his fellow prison mates were so young, just 17 and 18 year-old babies. they couldn't handle it, it broke them. but my grandfather was 30 so he had some life under his belt. more ability to use the kind of street smart logic that strengthens with age and age alone. and i think that played a huge part in his survival.

that and an unshakable faith that everything would turn out OK. despite the world around him being the most hopeless place on the planet.

oh, and he also was able to fuck with the japanese a little bit. he was a welder, an electrician by trade really, and he used to weld junk inside whatever equipment he was working on. this would make anything he was working on potentially break later on down the road. that's totally something i would do.

there's an episode of the show "the handmaid's tale" where offred (lead character) discovers a latin phrase written in her closet. it was left there by the handmaid who was captive in the house before offred replaced her. it translated into "don't let the bastards grind you down". i like to think that was etched on everything my grandfather welded. at least it was in his spirit.

he somehow survived some of the worst conditions a human being could ever endure. and then he went on to have a beautiful life. came home and married my grandmother and had an amazing family. i am sure the memories of his past haunted him like no one could imagine, but he still chose life. chose to live it while he was here. and made the absolute most of it.

* * *

a man in my family was an ACTUAL prisoner on planet earth, and yet here i am wallowing in a phil collins puddle that pales in comparison. i mean, there really is NO comparison.

and while i don't like to minimize anyone's own personal reaction to their own reality, i feel like this is a teachable moment. every single thing we endure on the spectrum of enduring things is a particle that sticks and makes us into who we are. why some people endure absolutely horrific things and others not so much is one of life's great mysteries. some think it might be our souls that chose what we go through because we wanted the challenge. others think it's completely up to chance. maybe it's bad karma from a past life. maybe it's just the (bad) luck of the draw. it's hard to know for sure. but the truth of it is that we all have to go through some awful shit in some way, shape, or form.

we can't cop-out. i mean, we CAN but then we pay for it. we wind up living a life half-lived. a life without consequences is a life without lessons learned. we stunt our growth. and that just simply isn't the point.

"take me home" is all about saying "i don't mind". i don't mind that the world fucks with me. i don't mind that the powers that be are constantly manipulating me and think i'm stupid. don't pity me for being a prisoner, i've been one forever and it's OK — i really don't care.

but the song also cries out in desperation for a chance to go home. because i just can't remember who i truly am. i can't remember the bigger picture. i don't get why i have to go through this.

the "i don't mind" of it all could be looked at as a sarcastic "it's fine." like that dumb shit women do when they don't want to admit that things are NOT fine.

but i don't hear that in the tone of the song.

i hear the "i don't mind" as more of a "i know that

everything is OK. i know that things suck. i know that i can get through it. i accept it all for what it is, and i don't mind."

and maybe "home" is that inner peace that is all you have in your deepest moments of crisis. the quiet space that is yours and yours alone. maybe "home" is where you retreat when you're tired of trying to remember. tired of trying to fight the system. tired of trying to get through the day with minimal spirit bruising.

maybe home is right HERE instead of THERE.

i'd imagine my grandfather had to create his own inner home out of nothing to stay sane as a prisoner. i am sure he visited that place as often as he could, and it was a temple of hope and light that he hung onto until the day he made it out of japan, safely back to his physical home in the states.

* * *

throughout awakening, we traverse the in-between. we get a taste of dimensions beyond the one we wake up in every morning. we uncover the truth about our multidimensional nature. it's easy to get lost in those magical parts of us to escape the mundane. the daily grind. the pain, the suffering, the injustice.

but we can't lose sight of the task at hand, which is learning how to make the everyday earth existence our home. because we are HERE, very much so. and the world is our playground, our school. it's the experience we signed up for. the good, the bad, and especially the ugly. we're alchemists of light and dark, just trying to accumulate as many points as possible before we leave this plane and get to analyze everything (which i'm both looking forward to and cringing over).

whenever i get the feeling that i want to go home, i remember i'm always home. wherever i am. take yourself home whenever you need to. you have the ability to create the home you think you need to escape to. it's all right here and it's all so perfect.

on ego death*

waking up
and shedding your ego
go hand in hand.

just like a snake has to shed layers of scales
to let the new layer come in,
you will undoubtedly be doing a whole lot of
shedding
as you get deeper
and deeper
into your awakening.

it's just part of the package.

i wish someone gave me a
heads up
about acute ego death before i experienced it
(the FIRST time).

and i don't mean give me a definition,
or simply tell me
that the concept exists,
because i really don't think that helps.

at the same time,
it's extremely difficult to
put into words what
it feels like.

but i'll do my best.

you might say,
"well, we're all shedding
constantly throughout our lives.
that's not a new concept".
and it isn't.

sure, we can all pinpoint times
where we've reinvented ourselves.

we change majors in college
when we decide to pursue something else.
we get divorces and
start new families.
we move to different places.
we feel good about these kinds of
self changes, because
they're 100%
completely under our control.

we're able to CHOOSE these changes,
and we feel empowered.

but what if your shedding snuck up on you?

what if you were
shedding behind the scenes
for a long time, and then

BOOM
you suddenly realize,
"wow, i'm fucking naked."

and now you're exposed.
and you didn't have time to plan it out,
so you have no idea what
you're supposed to be doing.

but you know you need clothes,
so you begin searching for
something to wear,
only to discover that
picking out an outfit
isn't so easy anymore.

you're in a closet filled with clothes
and hate everything.

it feels so
raw and
cold and
utterly humiliating.

you feel abandoned by YOU
because you come to the realization that
everything you were wearing
just didn't fit and
you were forcing yourself into some pretty ugly shit
for a really long time.

and the struggle between staying naked
and finding something to wear
is a battle that you thought
you only had to deal with before
getting ready
for a special event.

that's ego death.

adventure of a lifetime

on a flight to a work event, i wrote a musical to coldplay's greatest hits.

the inspiring song that formed the backbone of the story was "viva la vida". i pictured a man in a high-powered, white-collar job being absolutely rocked from a spontaneous spiritual awakening. seemingly all at once, his entire life as he knew it was stripped away from him. he didn't know who he was. he realized how many lives he destroyed in the name of corporate gains. how shitty he was to everyone. how much his wife hated him. how his kids despised him. and how he really didn't even know who they were. how all of the money he made never filled the gaping hole that was ultimate fulfillment. how he was so far away from god.

and so he fumbles through trying to reconcile it all, while chris martin sings and dances along in the background. he has an existential crisis to "clocks". he reconciles with his wife to "the scientist". he reconciles with his children to "fix you". he crafts his plan to save the rest of the world from a mundane life in the matrix to "every teardrop is a waterfall".

and he meets a spiritual guide to help him through it all. a beautiful, encouraging muse. a goddess in her own right. she appears to him like the ghosts appear to scrooge. a wake-up call that saves his life. a guardian angel who invites him to his new life. the "adventure of a lifetime".

i have high hopes that maybe someone from broadway will pick this up, because i still think about it multiple times a week.

post-flight and post-work trip, i decided to go to a past life regression at a little spiritual sanctuary i found, courtesy of the internet. an amazingly beautiful woman repurposed her home into a haven for spiritual seekers. she offered carefully curated experiences for a fucking bargain, if you ask me. i'm so grateful i was able to find her when i did.

the regression was in a group setting. there were maybe ten or so people there. and it was led by another amazing powerhouse of a woman — a shaman who specialized in past life regressions and plant medicine. she worked directly with the keepers of the plants down in south america, splitting her time between there and philly.

we all got comfy in our own little sacred spaces on the floor, aided by some colorful and welcoming pillows and yoga mats. and our gracious host was also an insanely gifted tibetan singing bowl maven. she provided the soundtrack for our impending journey to meet ourselves. it was all just too perfect.

we drifted into a deep meditative state, accompanied by the hauntingly beautiful bowl sounds and our shaman chanting and shaking instruments from a land far away. and before i knew it, i was somewhere else.

we were guided in our minds to walk down the long

hallway we came in on. guided to walk out of the door and into another world. a world where we'd be shown things that were hidden from us, due to eons of our DNA being fucked with. hidden on purpose from the powers that be, because if all of us remembered who we used to be, the world would heal itself overnight. so much power.

i walked into another room, a room where i would first be guided to remember something from my current life. a memory that would hold the first key to who i truly am. and what i walked into, i wasn't expecting.

i was in the kitchen, the kitchen of my parents' house where i grew up. it's been redone several times, but this version was a few back from its current state. a white and blueish tiled floor. cabinets with a creamy beige tint. country home inspired curtains and decor. and i was drawn to look at the counter.

there was a lonely glass of diet iced tea. and that was it. nothing else really to notice. we were guided to notice anyone else there, and there was no one. just me and a cold, sweaty glass of iced tea. i really struggled to understand why i was in THIS situation, out of all of the memories that could have been shown to me. this wasn't exciting at all. i was kinda pissed.

but then it hit me. i looked down at my hands. they were my 13-year-old hands. my body was my 13-year-old body. and that's when i noticed that i wasn't alone.

a glowing woman in white, with the most golden blonde

hair, seemed to come out of the tall pantry cabinet. and she looked at me with this look that instantly reminded me of the scene i was in.

this was the day that i decided that i was only going to have iced tea for breakfast. i wasn't going to eat.

my first conscious choice that kickstarted my eating disorder. my first conscious choice to abandon my true self. because i hated her. i was tired, tired of being bullied. hurt by mean girls picking on me. hurt from feeling like i had no control over wanting to explore who i wanted to become as a teenager. hurt from constantly comparing myself to britney spears.

and i started crying. uncontrollably. in both worlds i was straddling. the dream state and my 3D reality. i felt the tears, and then my guide reached out to me.

she looked at me with the biggest, most brilliant blue eyes and said to me, "this is where it stops. this is where you reclaim yourself. this is where you forgive yourself."

and then we were guided to leave this scene. to make peace with wherever we were because it was time to move on.

my guide took me by the hand and walked me through the biggest pantry cabinet in my parents' old kitchen, into the most picturesque fairy tale forest. narnia meets the legend of zelda.

we were guided to rest awhile. and so we sat on a mossy

rock by the most beautiful babbling brook. a tiger showed up and lay down beside me and let me pet it. i took a sip of the brook water and it tasted so clean, so crisp. i never wanted to leave. i seriously could have stayed there forever.

but it was time to go again. it was time to look at who i was beyond my current lifetime. this was what we were all waiting for, what we came for. and although i was still shaking like a leaf from what was just revealed to me, i knew i had to face what was next. i needed to remember because it was killing me not to. i needed this missing piece.

we walked out of the forest and through another portal. a mirror-like slice in the woods with a slimy, sparkly film that welcomed us in. and, just like that, the forest disappeared.

and so did my guide. i was now alone. and kind of afraid. we were guided to once again look around and notice our surroundings, who else was there, what was happening.

i was in a round room — no, a round tent. it had a dirt floor and walls covered with colorful flags. there were words on them in a language i both understood and wished i could understand. the tent had a high, circus-like ceiling, with smaller flags hanging off every angle.

who else was there? a man with the kindest face i have ever seen. he looked like he was of asian descent, and then i felt another wave of recognition wash over me. genghis khan came to mind, that time period, but who knows. and then i realized that this man was my partner, my rock. he looked at me with the most loving eyes, the most comforting gaze.

and then i realized that two small boys where on either side of him, grabbing at his clothes. my children. but why did they look so terrified? why were they crying?

we were guided to take note of who we were. i looked down at my hands again and noticed they were covered in jewelry, gold. i was wearing a magnificent purple and magenta colored dress, also adorned in gold. and my hair, oh my god my hair. it was black as night. thick, wavy. and smelled so so good, like i was washing it with some secret black market shampoo that was illegal, it smelled so great.

and i was twirling, dancing. while my husband looked at me adoringly, and my kids were hysterically crying. what in the actual fuck.

that's when the tent blew wide open. the main flap was carried away to reveal what was waiting for us outside. a complete hellscape.

it was night, the stars were glowing brighter than i have ever seen. the ground was dirt and getting kicked up, creating clouds that you couldn't see through. that's when i noticed it was being kicked up by horses, men on horses. warriors.

they had helmets on that covered their faces, but only down the middle. like a covering that shielded the nose and mouth, but left the eyes to see. and these guys were RIDING, i mean really riding the shit out of these horses.

brandishing weapons i have never seen before. i had no frame of reference for what they could have been, aside from them being really long and pointy, but not quite swords.

it was a chaotic scene. and it was also on fire.

fire was mixing with the dust so rapidly, and getting bigger and brighter.

i left the tent, still whirling and moving with the most perfect rhythmic grace, dancing to a beat that only i could hear. and i moved farther away from the tent, and closer to the chaos. men on horses crossing my path from both the left and the right, crying out in primal rage. like animals, beasts.

and onward i moved. the fires grew larger, higher. the dirt made it harder and harder to see. but still, i pressed on.

and then, like a cell splitting, i realized that i was now watching myself from the tent entrance. and i watched myself run straight into the fire. barefoot and brazen.

just in time for the shaman to guide us back home. back to our bodies, back down the hallway, and into the sanctuary space. i started to feel my fingers and toes again, felt my breath rising and falling. a comforting feeling to know that i was back, but also leaving me with this feeling of heartbreaking nostalgia, fearing that this experience would leave me as fast as my memories in this current lifetime.

i started to feel the soft light of the room touch my closed eyelids. and the vibrations of the singing bowls started filling my body, and the sounds poured back into my ears. our host's angelic voice, sporadically singing lyrics from popular songs as she was called. a true gift.

and as i was laying there, basking in the experience, she started to sing a song that brought me to a huge release. she started singing the words to "adventure of a lifetime".

i couldn't believe my ears. it was like she was co-writing my coldplay musical. it was like she merged with the guide who was helping me throughout my regression, and then it was as if we all merged into one great beam of light. i am finding it hard to express just how powerful this experience was with words. some experiences are simply beyond them.

after i fully came to, i couldn't stop crying. i was so grateful for the opportunity to catch a glimpse of who i've been. how much power i am really holding. and how beautiful of a synchronicity i was blessed to witness. once again, music has proved itself as my awakening guide. a portal to everything i need.

this lifetime so far has been an adventure i never saw coming. and it makes me constantly think about the lifetime that was revealed to me. how many more are just like it? will i ever remember them?

and then i realized that just because i can't remember them doesn't mean i don't carry them. they reveal themselves to me when i'm broken. when i don't think i can fight any longer. when i feel like giving up. when i lose hope that i'll ever see peace and justice and paradise. they reveal themselves to me in a language only my heart understands.

they help me turn a magic on that no one else has. they help me walk through the fire. they open my eyes to my soul and pave the road towards an ultimate greater destiny.

with every life i've led, i've become more refined. i shine brighter, i learn more. i touch others. i come home time and time again.

and while i have no idea if this current lifetime is my last as a human being, knowing that i've done this all before is all the solace i need to know that there's nothing here i cannot handle.

bitch

there is no one way to be.

let me repeat myself: there is no one way to be.

i'm not sure what happened to us in this new age of social media and personal brand and influencer absolute madness, but there is NO one way to be you. there's no guidebook. you're writing that every day yourself. there are no other authors.

and i am tired of the branded messaging that tells me to "BE YOU!" because it isn't genuine when it comes from someone who painstakingly went to great lengths to look completely perfect in the photo above the caption. like, stop sending me mixed messages. you're telling me to be ME, yet you're not being YOU. i can tell, and i am sorry if that's harsh.

i am not a brand. i'll never be one. i am me and that will change and morph along with my soul for the rest of my fucking life. i'm a human being, not a commodity. i am a fluid, free spirit floating on a rock through an ever-expanding universe.

there's so much advice given to people who are trying to "make it". don't curse or people won't want you on their stages. don't post a meme of george costanza because most people don't know who he is and they won't like it. make sure to use high res photos with your face clearly showing and make sure they're professionally done. make sure to write your posts with a script that's been proven for the most engagement. make sure to post x amount of times a day/week and if you can't, maybe you could hire someone to do it for you.

no. sorry, i'm just not fucking doing that. and if that's future fame suicide, then oh well. consider me never famous.

meredith brooks' "bitch" is the song i play every time i need to be reminded that i can be whatever i want, whenever i want. sometimes i'll listen to it on repeat until it really sinks in. because, some days, i want to just quit.

some days, i get so disillusioned with this world and my place in it. i get so beat up after scrolling through so many fake ass posts about what i should be doing and how i should look and who i should be listening to. oh, and also to "BE YOU!" it feels like getting shot with a zillion nails. it makes me want to scream. and sometimes i actually scream.

why are we in this place right now? how are we seemingly yelling from every angle to be the most authentic version of ourselves, but through this fucked up, warped, pre-made and pre-approved lens? it makes absolutely no sense to me.

i wish i could change it. and maybe i can. maybe a bunch of people will read this rant and stand up and be like "FUCK YEAH i hate that shit too."

but for now, i just want to say my piece and let the world

know where i stand.

i'll never conform. i've battled through HELL to get out of social prisons that told me who i could and couldn't be. it hurt so bad to live in them. i bore not only my own pain, but the pain of everyone else who had to put up with it too. i carried that pain for a long ass time. and then i let it go.

i'll never sell out. i don't care if someone came to my door RIGHT this second with a billion-dollar check that would be all mine if i just changed the way i wanted to express myself, even just a little bit. and believe me when i say i could really use a billion dollars right now. i could use a hundred dollars right now. i could use a ten dollar coupon code for grubhub right now.

i'll never bend to trends, critics, popularity. i lived a large chunk of my life under that oppressive regime and i fucking left. i'm not going back.

if i wake up and want to be a sexy goddess one day, awesome. if i wake up the next day and want to be an ugly wreck of a hag, i will. i might wake up and want to save the world and then get outside and be like, "yeah ya know what, not today. maybe not ever" and that's fine.

i don't want kids right now. but maybe someday i will and, if i do, i can have them in a perfect way that was destined to be and it will all be magical. and maybe i'll never want them and that's fucking magical too.

i've screwed up so many times. badly. but i have done SO much good in this life and i'll never stop trying. i stopped shaming myself for the bad times and decisions. when i feel guilty, i breathe in and out and pat myself on the back for MAKING it.

a lot of people love me. i know a few that hate my guts, and there's probably more that i think like me and they actually talk about how annoying i am over happy hour when i'm not there. and that's fine. i hate a lot of people too. life is like that.

i have numbed myself to what seemed like the point of no return, in the name of trying to be someone i wasn't. i tried so hard to kill whatever that was inside of me because it felt like a disease. why didn't i fit in? please just let me fit in. it's easier. i don't want to wake up feeling like this every day. i don't want to explore who i am so i can set myself free. i don't want people to mock me and think i'm crazy and lose friends and jobs and a comfortable life. but sometimes that's what happens when you and your higher self shake hands and say "let's do this."

numbing myself to it all was easy. until it wasn't. and so i revived myself. i woke the fuck up, bit the bullet, and am doing it anyway.

and i wouldn't want it any other way. and neither should you.

crazy

at some point in your awakening process, you'll brush up against the other-worldly. the unexplainable. the freaky shit.

the experiences that will make you question your sanity. the experiences that have sent a well-intentioned spiritual seeker to the nuthouse, diagnosed as schizophrenic, and pumped full of numbing meds. the experiences that you peek at inside a closed box and then realize that you can't just peek, you have to look at the whole thing and the lid blows open, and all of a sudden you're walking around in a world you don't recognize.

you're not crazy. i promise.

i was at the point at my last corporate job where i knew i wanted to leave, but didn't know how i was going to pull it off. i had started a couple of spare-time ventures and dabbled in side hustle. but nothing i was doing made me feel better about being stuck in my cubicle.

i was just starting to get into meditation and couldn't get enough. i tapped in instantly the moment i figured out how to calibrate myself enough to catch the frequency and hold on long enough to understand what all the hype was about. i was able to quiet my mind enough to start to gain access to the OTHER shit that you get when you meditate. the weird messages. memories that you have but don't know where they came from. glimpses of past lives.

glimpses of future ones. reminders to call someone you haven't thought about in ages. flickers of inspiration for my next big idea. keys that unlocked the answers i needed.

and all i wanted to do at work was tune out, but that was impossible. someone always needed something stupid. some executive was always on my ass about something. none of it mattered, but my paycheck did. so i played the game as best as i could. it was hard.

on one particular summer afternoon, i was sitting in my cube and, all of a sudden, i started feeling hot, which was my first hint that something was off. the AC was always blasting at a constant like 50 degrees and i had a space heater on all year round. why the fuck can't we regulate commercial office space temperatures?

i started sweating, got dizzy. jittery. did i have too much coffee? not enough coffee? it was like 2pm, i was done my coffee for the day. am i sick? i never get sick.

i started looking around to see if my coworkers noticed my silent secret freak out. no one did.

and then i started to literally lose my mind. like, i kinda started blacking out. i did exactly what i shouldn't have done and started web MD-ing my symptoms. a psychotic break. that's what kept coming up. i started panicking.

but i was sane! i knew i was sane. i wasn't going to take a web MD diagnosis at face value. i also knew what it was like to go insane and have gone insane several times throughout life and this just wasn't the same. it wasn't it.

i texted a spiritual seeking friend of mine and told her what was going on. she told me i wasn't crazy. she told me to google "kundalini awakening". i did. i had no idea what the hell that was.

there are many definitions and explanations and i encourage you to do your own research and find one that best fits you. awakening is not a one size all deal, no matter how many instagram coaches try to tell you otherwise for just four installments of $222.

to me, i took it as a crossing of some sort, a threshold i finally leaped over. i had been taking stock of my life for six years prior, gradually asking questions, undoing, relearning, rethinking. taking stock of how i fuck up, how i let others take advantage of me. realized i wasn't living the life i was meant to live. realized my soul wouldn't let me off the hook anymore.

and sometimes your soul shows you "it's time to shine" in the strangest, most fascinating ways.

anyway, i found some articles. ironically, the symptoms of a kundalini awakening were the same as a psychotic break, fancy that.

reading all of this didn't do anything to alleviate my hot flashes and shaking. in fact, they were getting worse. i once again looked around me and thought for SURE my coworkers were going to catch me going all batshit nuts, drenched in my own pool of sweat.

"get up. go outside." a voice from both nowhere and

everywhere. so that's what i did.

it felt like my feet weren't even hitting the ground as i walked to the elevator. i passed several people and they didn't have faces. i looked at my hands and they didn't look like my hands. holy fuck, i think i'm going to pass out.

the same elevator ride i took day in and day out, 17 floors, felt like one floor and a thousand floors at the same time. my stomach was in knots, full of butterflies. i just wanted relief.

i got to the bottom and off the elevator. every tiny noise in the lobby had an echo. it was so goddamn loud. everything was zooming in and out. did someone lace the water cooler with LSD? they must have. but then everyone else would feel like me. oh yeah, kundalini. i forgot.

"go to the park." the park across the street? OK, no problem.

i left the building, and the light was so bright, i almost couldn't handle it. and just when i thought i was regaining some composure, the world stopped around me. everything turned into the most beautiful, fantastical, real-life comic book. the people who i usually get so annoyed at walking in the park looked like my best friends. i started laughing.

puppies playing and i didn't notice their leashes. i looked up at the sun. it was lined up with the street perfectly, and it looked like it was moving around like a fairy. i couldn't stop laughing. the grass started waving to me. the birds were singing the best songs i've ever heard.

there was a street fair going on. so many vendors. they all looked like cartoon characters. everyone was so happy. were they really happy? this was a movie, right? am i watching a movie? am i in the movie?

i walked up to a random booth because all i could see were shapes and colors. then i realized they were chocolates. artisan chocolates with geometric patterns on them. i bought some. they were so fucking expensive.

i ate one as i watched the park behind me turn into an impressionist painting. i found a bench and sat down. just stared. it was pure bliss. i couldn't believe it.

"go back inside, you asshole."

oh my god, i had no clue how long it had been. i randomly just left my desk to trip out unexpectedly. was it hours? i didn't know. i didn't have my phone on me. did i have a meeting? oh shit, i'm missing a meeting. wait, i don't have any meetings today.

i started to snap out of it. i sat on the park bench and watched the world go back to "normal". i wasn't in a painting. i was across the street from my lame-ass office. what a bummer.

i went back inside and was shocked to realize i had only been gone for a half an hour. no one was looking for me. no meetings.

i brought back some of the chocolates i didn't eat. probably gave some away, i don't remember. i definitely couldn't concentrate anymore.

what the fuck did i just experience? i went back to the kundalini articles. and then i looked at other articles. i couldn't quite find an explanation for what i experienced. and that's when i realized that there wasn't anything written about what i experienced because my experience was mine only. no one before me experienced it and no one would ever experience it after me. it was unique. it was my higher self showing me something i needed.

i didn't understand it right away. and that's kind of how awakening works. something happens to you but you don't know why it's happening in the moment. it's meant for you to chew on it as you fumble through life until you put the pieces together. and you always will. awakening is outside of time and space. it's non-linear. it's a constant spiral of ups and downs and insides out.

i mustered up the courage to leave my corporate job a few months later. and i always come back to the experience i had that day in the park. it was almost as if it was supposed to reveal to me that there was so much more here. so much to see and do and experience. it peeled back the overlay that is our society, the burdens we put on ourselves. it lifted the veil on the matrix that binds us to the things that don't matter and distracts us from the things that do.

it was a little treat for me because i had worked so hard up until that point at trying to figure out what it all meant, why i was here. a little token of appreciation from the universe for going balls deep in taking off the suit of inauthenticity that had been dragging me down for the better part of my 33 years on planet earth.

* * *

gnarls barkley's "crazy" came out the year before i finished college. summer-ish 2006. i was 21.

it was all over the radio. it was our drinking song. our pregame song. whenever i'd hear the first initial beats, i'd get so pumped. i had just finished an intensive eating disorder treatment program, was full of antianxiety/ antidepressant meds and high off group therapy kumbaya. "crazy" was second on my list of mental patient anthems, after amy winehouse's "rehab". i took pride in being a crazy, mentally unstable bitch.

and i still do. you can't really say you've lived unless you've gone crazy. there's magic in the madness. you don't awaken unless you break. you can't have one without the other.

i heard a stripped-down, female cover of "crazy" more recently and realized it was much more than a drinking anthem. it's an awakening anthem. for everyone who loses touch with reality in the name of saving their soul. no one ever said that waking up to who you are is going to look like something you've seen before. you can't compare it to anything else.

those who know, know. and to those who haven't experienced the sheer craziness of awakening yet, if you're open to it and want it, it's coming. and it will hit you when you least expect it.

when you're driving. cooking. playing with your children.

sitting in your cubicle, wishing you were anywhere else. and then your wish comes true. you can handle it. you're not the bad kind of crazy.

you're the truth.

so much more*

for those who peeked behind the curtain of their everyday lives
and caught a glimpse of something other-worldly.

for those who dipped a toe into the possibility that unfolds
as you express yourself as you really are.

for those who inherently understand that
life as we all know it is just the surface
of an endless ocean
of wonder and awe.

for those who hopped off the hamster wheel of
society's pressure and drive,
expecting to have the worst FOMO,
but were blissfully surprised.

for those who have battled their demons
and won, only to question
"is this all there is?"

no.

there's so much more.

and it's waiting for you.

it's been waiting for you
since the beginning of life
as you know it.

yikes

kanye west is an awakening archetype.

i've followed him his entire career and have always
admired his cocky confidence. his outbursts. him calling
out george bush was one of my favorite moments in MTV
video music award show history. that and his ambush of
taylor swift. i'm team kanye all the way.

many people will say he's devolved since his old music. i
feel like i've even seen "i miss the old kanye" on t-shirts.
i'm guilty of saying it myself. but the older i get and the
older he gets, the more i understand him.

he's unapologetically kanye west. doesn't give a fuck if you
think his latest album about jesus sucks. he doesn't care
because he needed to express it. spirit needed it to come
through him. he doesn't care if you wipe your ass with his
music. in fact, if enough people did, he'd probably
capitalize off making some kind of kanye west poopity
scoop toilet paper. and that's why i love him.

he's a genius. ahead of his time. there's no one like him
now and no one like him will follow. i feel insanely
privileged to live on an earth that includes kanye west.
because i see myself in him.

i channel him whenever i want to stop writing. whenever i
think about no one caring about what i have to say. "what
would kanye do?" you know what he'd do? he'd put out

that song that no one likes. and he'll laugh the entire time at the reactions. laugh all the way to the fucking bank.

the muses work through him. he's just a conduit. and that's the ultimate aspiration. to be a clear channel to transmit things to the masses so that they stop and think. they might not always like what they hear, but they don't forget it. and that's the whole point. no press is bad press. no bad song is really a bad song if people can't shut up about how bad it is. how controversial something is. the unbelievable thing you can't believe kanye said is probably just what you needed.

"yikes" is on my playlist because, to me, it's the essence of kanye. there are so many stories about him having mental breakdowns. disappearing for a while. dyeing his hair when he comes back out in public. where did he go? that's up for debate. but i'd like to think that "yikes" came out of one of his breakdowns. the best art always does.

i see myself in kanye and "yikes" in particular because it sums up the essence of a mental insanity experience, of which i've experienced a few. it's scary as fuck. you can feel the most alive you've ever felt and the farthest away from yourself at the same time. you run for help the first time it happens because you don't know what else to do. and they put you on medication.

medication that helps you level off but then you lose your edge. the muses stop visiting as often. you know you're still inside but you can't come out to play. this is why a lot of people eventually stop taking them. they crave the highs that come with the lows.

i'm not knocking anyone who takes psych meds. i know plenty of people who can't survive without them. but i know, personally, that i can't be myself on them. it was cop-out for me. i'm so fucking crazy by design. a lot of us are. and i think it's an insane person's mission to somehow tame the beast and show people a new way.

you scare yourself when you realize you're crazy and whole-heartedly embrace it. it's fucked up! people stop understanding you the way they used to. they become concerned. ask you if you're OK. and while you know you're not, you can't tell them that. it's like you have to be crazy all by yourself and live a double life, lest you be involuntarily committed.

unfortunately for kanye, hollywood doesn't really prefer people showing their crazy. which is why i love him so much. every time he "goes away", he comes out embracing himself even more. and i say that with the utmost reverence. do you understand how much guts that takes? go down the rabbit hole of hollywood mind-control conspiracy theories and DM me some time.

fortunately for the rest of us, we're allowed to walk around crazy within some reasonable parameters. in fact, if you've been blessed with the crazy, you're responsible for using it for the public's benefit. think about it. would the universe create you as anything short of perfect?

your insanity is your superpower.

and the demons will undoubtedly come after you if you're crazy. they'll try to tempt you away from your genius with booze and pills. make you into a sex addict. they'll come to you in the form of toxic relationships that force you into showing the world your unrefined crazy. the kind of crazy that puts you in danger of getting put away in a straitjacket.

this is what the demons want. they thrive off the world not seeing your crazy, because they know it's what humanity needs.

so, in spite of it all, it's your mission to be crazy anyway. fumble through it. learn it. master it. it's the most amazing gift you could ever possess. the more people call you crazy, the more of a force to be reckoned with you are.

in a sea of taylor swifts, be a kanye.

chandelier

there's a nightclub in the philly gayborhood that's known for staying open much later than most other places, great dance music, an all-around fantastic environment to not give a fuck. i was kicked out one night for falling asleep at the bar, then trying to order another drink. they also sometimes had a hot dog griller with free hot dogs (i mean, i THINK they were free. if not, i'm really sorry i was just taking them). i don't remember what they taste like, but i know i've had several. and that pretty much sums up my life at the time i was frequenting this place. had way too much of something that's really bad for you, but having little to no recollection.

the place had the best music ever. i was really into indie electronic at the time and they'd have DJs who were absolute fire. i remember about a year or so later, once i hung up my 24/7 party hat, i heard sia's "chandelier" for the first time — a remix of it actually. it always made me wish that i'd heard it for the first time while i was at the club, at approximately 3:13am, coming out of a blackout, and looking for a hot dog. it was the perfect wasted bitch anthem.

at first, i heard it superficially. took the lyrics for what they were. and then eventually, i started to read more into it. and then i felt it. felt the somber tone of it. felt the shakiness. the pain of someone who won't look their shadow in the face. the portrait of the celebrity who commits suicide and everyone is just dumbfounded because they never saw it coming. the person who's the life of the party and not much else is known about them, out of respect for everyone who'd find out they're just another boring piece of shit. the person who doesn't care about tomorrow because hidden within is the secret whisper that they probably wouldn't hate it if they didn't wake up.

holding on for dear fucking life, yet singing their heart out. with such a thick, silky bravado. and isn't that a portrait of humanity?

most people have a sort of teenage rebellion to come of age, but i decided to have my own version of an amish rumspringa at 26. i moved into a tiny studio apartment in a pretty posh area of the city after breaking up with the person everyone thought i was going to marry. good on paper, picture-perfect, look up "upstanding man who will take care of you forever" and his photo's there. but that fucking scared the shit out of me. i didn't yet know that's not what i wanted in a relationship, but i knew i felt completely suffocated. i also was horrible at really expressing my feelings and was the queen of blindsiding breakups. so, he got blindsided.

the night i moved into my new place really marked the start of what would wind up being the most destructive, catalytic chapter of my life. i decided to try on an outfit i always fantasized about but was never allowed to wear: the full out party girl. that night I moved in, i had my fling at the time over and we got hammered, went to some bars. he left a beer in the freezer too long and it exploded. i

drank a magnum bottle of wine and threw up. we were
listening to fleetwood mac and arguing over who was
better: christine or stevie. it was also a sunday, which
meant a hungover sick monday.

but it wasn't so bad. the office i worked in at the time had
a little deli in the basement run by this little ball of fire
named ruth who would make you a bacon egg and cheese
that could kill any fucking ailment you can think of. ruth
has literally seen me at my absolute worst, now that i'm
thinking about it. more than anyone. anyway, i slowly got
used to the hangovers. they got less and less bothersome.
and i went out more and more nights.

i started a ritual where i'd go to the liquor store maybe
twice a week and buy three olives grape vodka. every time
i opened it, i would sit on spotify and script playlists that
felt like a magnum opus. i felt like a fucking maestro. mid-
shelf grape vodka does that to a person.

and i started drinking alone. and more often.

and then came all of the "friends". i met some really
fucking odd people. slept with odder. i'd have these
romantic relationships that would come in so hot and then
crash and burn harder and faster than they arrived. i
would meet these gal pals who'd just completely captivate
me with what seemed like fearlessness, but was really a
cover for an addiction or daddy issues or BPD. and i'm
sure i related to them so hard because so much of that was
me too. those friendships would leave as fast as the men
did. or i'd get rid of them faster than they could leave. like i

was constantly playing this game of building up something to the pinnacle point, and then actively destroying it. like a kid who builds a lego tower only to kick it down like a maniac.

i was really lonely. really broken. i'll never forget what it was like to sit in that apartment, drunk. by myself. one time i laid in bed for the entirety of a sunny, beautiful saturday with the curtains drawn, a bottle of wine, and watched like three seasons of intervention by myself. and ate a box of reduced-fat cheeze-its.

and one time some dude didn't call me back so I downed half a bottle of vodka, called a neighbor i barely knew, and went to a tattoo shop. i didn't even know what i was going to get before i got there. decided on a quote from bukowski on my left side rib cage, because that's where he would've loved to have seen it. "what matters most is how you walk through the fire" in impeccable, exquisite script. it hurt so bad, even though i was already numb.

i was so busy. i filled almost every night i could with something to do, somewhere to go. i started getting into adderall to help me stay up. fucking black magic. i remember taking it during work for a week straight and it made writing shitty pointless emails worth it. i remember going to an amazing party at this korean banquet hall and getting up on stage with the DJ and feeling like i was invincible. i remember running into someone from college who i hadn't seen since graduating and like, immediately falling in love. i remember screaming something so silly and my friend who i came with got so embarrassed. and then she took this amazing picture of me. i thought it was facebook profile pic worthy. she told me i had adderall eyes.

i got so wasted in that apartment that one time i fell asleep while boiling kraft mac n cheese and forgot about it. i also disabled my smoke alarm and so i woke up to smoldering air and my smoldering forgotten snack.

the apartment was so old and it definitely had an old smell. but i grew to like it. like old books and history. it didn't have rats in it that i knew of. BUT actually, now that i'm remembering, the girl who lived in the other apartment had sick dogs who used to shit all over and that smell was NOT good. but it wasn't all the time. and the dogs were nice. someone else who lived upstairs had a golden retriever that found its way into my apartment once while i went to take out the trash. oh, and sometimes, i would open my window and throw my trash bags out into the dumpster of the complex next door. sometimes i'd miss and it made me laugh so hard every time. alone.

i remember getting locked out once after walking by the river and having to sit on my steps until someone from another apartment came home. and it was hours. i would sit on the stoop at night and read trash tabloids until it got chilly and too dark to see. i once sat on that stoop after a frank ocean concert and passed out while waiting for someone to come over. not sure how long i was sitting there. i also emailed out of work that next day. i remember reading in between the lines of my boss's response, knowing that he knew i wasn't really sick, and had terrible anxiety that whole next day.

i got into a terrible fight in my apartment once, with a guy i was seeing. he brought out the worst in me, and i'm sure i did in him too. in a grape vodka-filled rage, i screamed at him. he left. i punched the old-ass wood floor of that apartment repeatedly, so hard i almost broke my hand. and he came back in after about 20 minutes because he was on the other side of the door the entire time, listening to me have a complete breakdown. he came back in. i forgave him. then broke up with him. then got back together with him. then broke up with him.

the apartment had these built-in shelves that i always pretended were a fancy curio cabinet. it had a small oven that i barely used. i hardly ever cooked there. one, rare time, i walked to this fancy grocery store to buy ingredients to make this fancy dinner for myself, taking a crack at the self-care shit i'd read in cosmo. the dinner was great. but then i spent the rest of the night crying because i didn't have anyone to share it with. and drank a bottle of wine. probably two.

there was a little coffee shop around the corner where i'd go to try to work on my master's thesis on weekend mornings, but would always wind up staring out the window and ordering more coffee until i got antsy enough to go home and switch to beer. there was a pizza place around another corner that i'm pretty sure was run by some kind of eastern bloc mob. i'd take my grad school work there and sit outside and the owner would come out and give me shots of tequila. i really don't wonder at all why my advisor ripped me a new one at that breakfast meeting. she told me that she was going to extend me an extra semester because what i had as drafts were so far from graduation material.

i mastered the art of sleep-driving on i76 west, my commute to work. the traffic was always so so bad, but on most mornings, i lived for the part where i'd come around towards city ave and slowly grind to a halt. nod off and go a bit, nod off, go.

my car would always get towed too. mostly because i'd park it like an asshole. one time i went looking for my car to go to work and realized it was towed. i had the guy who drove me to punch a wood floor take me to the impound lot and i didn't have enough money or credit to get the car out. he paid for the whole thing. and then took me to boston market. their cornbread is so fucking good.

there were so many great bars. they all felt like home to me, even more than the apartment. i met this amazing guy once at one of my favorite bars the night of his 30th birthday. we met through friends and he was alone, in between celebratory places. i thought we were destined to be together forever. a psychic i saw regularly would always say his name to me. and then i found out he had a girlfriend. every time i go to that bar i think of that. oh, and i never forget the bar with carpet that had a party the night of the oscars.

there was another bar which has a special place in my heart because it was the first bar i went to alone. i remember asking an older friend if that was a loser thing to do, and she told me to just keep checking the door as if you're waiting for someone. so that's what i did. (side note: i also always think of this bar when i hear mazzy star's "fade into you" because it was playing that night.) i wound up becoming momentary best friends with a woman who was waiting for her younger boyfriend to show up. she told me all about how much he beat her and how she wasn't sure how she was going to leave him. and then when he showed up, the three of us did several shots. i don't remember how i got home.

one night, a guy who i had no business messing around with anymore randomly texted me "be ready in 20 minutes" and i remember scrambling around my apartment, trying to take a fast shower with the shitty water pressure and still had shampoo in my hair when i ran out of the house. he took me to a dive bar. another guy came over for valentine's day. i broke out in tears because he made me feel like an asshole for starting up the "so what are we" talk. said he didn't want to BE anything and enjoyed the casual thing we had going. they all enjoy the casual thing you have going. then he told me that i looked pretty when i cried. he also tried to blame me for giving him a rash that wound up being shingles. i think i invited him over like months later because he wanted to apologize.

i remember finding a bug so big i think it started talking to me in perfect english. i freaked the fuck out and smacked it, and it flew down the drain. then it came back a week later and i smashed it, but not enough to kill it. just enough to whack one of its antennae off and enough for it to stick on my wall for the rest of my lease.

everyone at work would be so intrigued with my stories. they'd hang on my every word when i'd recount what happened to me on any given monday night because it was always dramatic and always drunk. my work mom would always tell me i'd meet someone someday who would be my prince. and honestly, she probably wanted me to settle the fuck down so she could sleep at night.

i went to so many shows. so many parties. just partied so fucking hard. i mean, i'm still super extroverted and still love to party, but jesus christ, i'm not sure how i lived through that time of my life. even remembering this shit takes it out of me. i think because every time i remember, a piece of me relives it. every single moment. of every memory really, but this time of my life holds a really special place in my heart.

i'd spend most of the years after this time being really embarrassed about it. feeling really sorry and guilty. sorry for hurting a lot of people and guilty for hurting myself. i think the guilt was worse. and the shame, man. the utter fucking shame that cripples you to the core. the kind of shame that's supposed to be reserved for the world's worst criminals, yet somehow it's stuck on you. peeling off the shame feels like chipping away at an old gel manicure. you can't fully peel it off without taking some of the nail with you.

i really was holding on for dear life during that time. i didn't want to face what i needed to face, which was that i didn't know who i was. that apartment was a limbo space for me. the space that came after shedding the me that was a pile of social conditioning and catholic guilt, but the space before honoring my higher self's voice for the first time. not quite the incubation period, but a lobby to somewhere much greater. it was more of a holding cell with padded walls that allowed me to sweat it out before building. a baptismal font, filled with alcohol.

a therapist told me i'm a master at avoiding pain. and while it's not something people are proud of, it should be something to marvel at. how human beings are capable of numbing out and avoiding the necessary because it hurts. it burns. and it leaves massive scars. how somehow we've evolved into being the most addicted and avoidant that we've ever been. and i can't help but to think, as i wonder why, that maybe it's because we're at a point in our evolution where we're being called to come home. called home to who we really are, louder than we've ever been called. i don't think it's a coincidence.

i wanted to be who everyone called for a great time. wanted to be loved and noticed. and praised. and honored. i wanted to feel free. i wanted to wear a permanent shield on my face that was tear-proof. i wanted to freefall from the rafters into a void and hold that feeling as long as possible.

but there's always a crash. always.

i couldn't swing forever because, while an object in motion stays in motion, it eventually gains enough momentum to start knocking into shit. destroys shit. you have to hop off so you don't throw up. and i threw up everywhere. at the end of the ride, i couldn't pay my rent. i put one of my credit cards over the limit buying grape vodka. that was one of many wake up calls.

i don't think the gravity of what i went through during that time hit me until about a year or so ago. it's way more than a story of someone who "turns their life around". that's so mainstream motivational. i went through what i went through to liberate myself. it looked like a hot fucking mess, but it was the cleanest and most thorough baptism one could go through. and if you find yourself in this story, know that's what you went through too. no one comes out of this journey unscathed. but everyone comes out clean if they allow it.

you're allowed to look down and open your eyes. and even if you can only hold onto tonight, keep holding on. honor it all. the shame and the hangovers and the fucked up decisions you make and the great ones you didn't make.

if you listen really close to chandelier during the chorus, underneath sia belting it out, you can hear a softer sia, gently singing along like it's another version of her in a car somewhere on a lonely highway.

that softer version is me now. i never noticed it until i sat down to write this.

and how fucking powerful is that? to be able to relive a painful scene from life and gently sing alongside of the wounded version of yourself.

that is growth.

fun fact*

fun fact:
some people in your life like you just the way you are,
like billy joel.

some of them wouldn't be able to handle it
if you decided to do a complete 180
from what they're used to.

they'll tell you they're concerned.
they'll do things to keep you the way you are because
it's more comfortable.
they might sabotage whatever it is you're setting out to do
and they might not even realize they're doing it.

or maybe it's YOU that can't deal with the discomfort
of people thinking you're crazy
so you don't go after what you really want.
because fighting with people really sucks.
because you don't want to rock any boats.
because you care about people deeply and
putting your own needs on the back burner seems easier.

but you know deep down that
you're always going to have that burning desire
to be who you really are.
to let that version of you run wild
and live the way you were meant to live.

so live that way.

the right people in your life won't care
that you're evolving.
the right people will welcome your growth because they
know
they'll be able to learn something from you, too.
keep those people and
discard the rest.

and if i can muster up the strength to
speak my out-of-this-world truth,
so
can
you.

(that walkout song)

i couldn't focus at all at work that thursday. i was pretty much doing the bare minimum required every day anyway, but i was just too excited. it was the kind of day where i had to put a post-it over the clock in the corner of my laptop because it would freeze for ten hours whenever i looked at it, making the day drag like no other.

i was heading to my first "big spend" woo-woo spiritual event, held by a really big name (who i'll refer to as RBN from here on out) the next day. it was a weekend thing and i was going by myself. i love doing things by myself and always have, but this felt different. it almost felt like i was going to some kind of initiation. getting a notch in my spiritual seeking belt because i had reached a new level of figuring it all out, whatever that means.

i spent the next day travelling to my destination and walked around town a bit when i arrived. checked into the boutique hotel i'd overspent on. found a crystal shop and bought some crystals i knew (and still know) jack shit about, but felt like they were giving me some kind of jolt that i needed. and then i headed over to the kickoff night of the event. it was such a pretty evening too. the sun was setting so perfectly and the part of town i was in had just the right tree-to-building ratio to make me forget about how uncomfortable any big city outside my familiar philadelphia makes me.

in the line to check in, i met some amazing people. all spiritual seekers like me, wanting to figure out how to capitalize on the gifts that god gave them. i was so insecure about my business idea at the time, but acted like it was already a million-dollar production. i faked the confidence to fit into conversations, which everyone else was obviously doing too. and then i met an amazing woman who also wanted to quit her job to pursue a life of freedom and magic. we became fast friends. and we're still friends today!

once check-in was over, we all headed into the meeting space. the lobby was filled with all kinds of goodies that RBN probably had a partnership with — fancy workout clothes for purchase, free high-end water, the latest and greatest in trendy health food brands. i was really impressed. then i picked up my goodie bag filled with even more treats and the token workbook that comes with every self-development adventure.

i shuffled in with my new friend and we grabbed great seats. met more amazing women. i was just buzzing. i felt like i'd found a new home and i was about to be reborn with RBN as my doula. i just knew that being in their presence would be the thing i needed to figure out what i was really supposed to be doing in life. RBN was the answer to all of my prayers, the solution to all of my spiritual crises. i mean, this person was so well known and so well off and so well liked, that HAD to mean i was in the right place.

and then the lights went down. a DJ who could have been an archangel incarnate started playing (that walkout song) and out walks RBN.

people lose their shit. they're crying. i'm crying. and clapping. and crying. and dancing that fucked up awkward dance you do when you're in a stadium seat. you know, the one that makes you look like a 70-year-old white lady with bad knees.

RBN was glowing. a stunning, magnetic, presence. the opening talk felt like a jolt of holy lightning through my body. and then came the guided meditation. i never really meditated in my life before because i could never turn my mind down enough. but here i was, chanting some sanskrit wonder jibberish next to my new soul clan. crying away. releasing all kinds of shit i didn't know i was holding onto.

when i opened my eyes, i looked around at the rest of the audience. everyone was wiping away tears and gently nodding to the person next to them, sometimes with a little hand squeeze. it was a truly magical experience.

and then i looked to the other side of the room at the staff that was on standby. they looked...uneasy.

i figured OK, events are stressful. i knew that feeling very well from my own corporate event planning experiences. the event kicks off without a hitch, but you're thinking it's too good to be true. and then eventually you calm down once you see things are going smoothly.

but they just weren't calming down. my energy spidey-senses were going off the rails like a crazy train. it was really distracting. it was like the whole team was waiting for RBN to explode. they all seemed so concerned with how RBN was going to react at all times.

and then i started to look at RBN to see where this could have been stemming from. was RBN really a mean person in real life? a tyrant in spiritual sheep's clothing? a sham? i didn't think so. i didn't WANT to think so. i tried to brush it off but kept finding myself scrutinizing RBN, trying to catch them in the very act that the staff was on the edge of their seats waiting for.

and then, i saw it.

the room full of attendees would start buzzing at every break. and why wouldn't it? it was filled to the brim with a bunch of spiritual hopefuls, all learning so much about how to become the best, awakest, most profitable version of themselves. we couldn't help but turn to our neighbors and trade breakthroughs.

and pull out our phones and text updates to everyone back home. and answer missed calls. staying plugged in.

but it was also difficult to corral everyone back into RBN's presentations after every break. it's natural for people to need to settle back into attention. especially when we're all acting like excited kids on a class trip, seeing things for the first time.

RBN wasn't a fan of this problem. they'd get increasingly more and more tense after every break, and you could read it in their voice. getting increasingly more and more like that teacher that has to scold you back into paying attention.

and then RBN kinda lost it. in the middle of their almighty stage presence that was captivating the third eyes of the audience, they snapped. made a couple of petty remarks in a tone that made me fucking cringe. i looked at my new bestie next to me and we made eye contact, and instantly i knew she was cringing too.

and then i looked back at the staff and knew for certain that this was the storm they knew was coming. they immediately started whispering and scrambling and were one fidget away from running around like chickens without heads.

my heart sank. like, completely deflated. how could this be?

RBN was the first spiritual leader that made sense to me. the one i put all of my trust in to help bring me to the next level of my awakening. i spent so much money on books and this seminar and put all my chips on black. RBN was supposed to save me. RBN was more than human.

except they weren't.

RBN was a human just like me. a flawed being, who gets pissed off at other humans as much as the next one. but i couldn't deal with it. it just couldn't be happening.

when the weekend came to a close, we all got parting gifts, more swag. but somehow, it wasn't as exciting as it was when i got there on friday. it all just felt so fake. so artificially forced.

but there was still the meet and greet! i'd get a chance to actually meet RBN, have some face time. and surely, when i was up close and personal with them, i'd be able to feel the vibes and reaffirm their higher-than-human presence.

but when it was my turn to get my 1:1 handshake and thank you, i looked RBN dead in the eyes and saw an ordinary human. it was almost like looking in a mirror. i saw myself in RBN. saw someone who was just trying to enlighten others in the best way they knew how. someone who still fights with their demons, despite having a halo glow and a multi-million dollar business.

i made my way back home and sat with my newfound cognitive dissonance. it felt like absolute shit. if this spiritual leader wasn't "it", did that mean i had to find a new one? surely there must be leaders out there that could give me what i was looking for. that infallibility that made me forget about my own. a new benchmark to measure my awakening against. a being who would be able to really hand me the keys to the kingdom.

and so i kept on searching. and i'd find new leaders to follow, who would ultimately all fall from grace and let me down. it took a huge slap in the face in the form of a leader showing me some real shitty true colors for me to stop. a slap that took me out of seeking completely.

in hindsight, i wish that i would have seen the lesson in my experience with RBN, but i also know that the universe doesn't lift a lesson until you really understand it. and so i'm grateful for how i eventually got there.

you'll never move forward in your awakening journey if you're putting it in the hands of another human being. by all means, learn as much as you can from the people that set off a resonant tone in your soul. but don't put them on a pedestal expecting them not to fall.

as far as i know, there aren't any human beings that don't make mistakes. even really enlightened ones. and if any of them try to tell you that they don't get triggered anymore, they're above humanity, or anything else that feels like they're separate from you — run the fuck away in the other direction.

no matter where you are in your spiritual quest, don't ever abandon your intuition. don't ever doubt its power, no matter how shoddy you think it is, or how many times you've ignored it.

that's the beauty of discernment. it's like a fine wine. gets better and better with time.

and if your own RBN has fallen from grace and you're having a multidimensional meltdown, know that they're just a mirror.

know that you're way more powerful than you give yourself credit for.

know that you have all of the answers inside of you, nowhere else.

follow, but don't get lost. admire, but don't worship. be moved, but not to the point where you've moved so far from your center and off your path. we're all walking different paths. and the walking never stops.

learn from those you can walk alongside.

and learn the most from yourself.

thank u

i was on my way home from a trip to denver, on the train to the airport, and i randomly felt like listening to alanis morrisette. i downloaded a playlist of her greatest hits.

i had just finished a long weekend with an amazing group of people at a conference on public speaking. i had (and still have) a burning desire to share my stories with people on stage. at the time, i wanted to create a talk about leaving corporate america, in the hopes that it would inspire others to do the same.

i maxxed out a credit card springing for the full package, which included a photoshoot, hair and makeup, and a custom promo video of your talk. i was so nervous. this was it. i better not fuck it up.

i read the draft of my talk on the plane ride to the event and i felt sick to my stomach. it wasn't "me". it was full of clichés, shit i picked up from instagram boss babe coaches, a hodgepodge of the personalities i worshipped within the self-development space. so lame and so inauthentic.

i rewrote the entire thing on that plane ride. and then rewrote it again at the actual event. and then again right before i had to go on stage where they would record my video. even then, i didn't think it was 100% me, but i went for it. and i got such glowing reviews. i even won the first prize where i won a trip back to do the conference again for free. to write more amazing talks.

i left the event on a high note, but i still felt so fake. what was wrong with me? why wasn't i getting it? why was being myself so goddamn hard? it hurt like hell.

* * *

when i put alanis on during that train ride, i took myself back to a place when i was really young — when "you outta know" came out. i remember chuckling when someone older than me told me it was about uncle joey from full house.

i remember riding in my aunt's car listening to NPR and someone was interviewing alanis when she released "jagged little pill". i was like ten years old and a lot of it went over my head, but i knew she was going to be important. knew she was going to leave a much-needed mark on this world.

there was something about her i instantly admired. i remember her "ironic" music video, where she was dressed up as a bunch of different personalities of herself, all riding in the same car, and i related to that BIG TIME.

i remember going to a sleepover party for a friend's birthday and getting made fun of because i didn't know who the spice girls were, and i still hadn't seen "clueless". i felt like such a loser.

but i did know who alanis was. and to me, she was cooler than any manufactured pop robot.

she was sort of a hero for underdog girls growing up in the

90s. she was true to herself and a welcome contrast to all of the cookie-cutter girl groups that were coming out in droves. i was in an in-between state back then, in between wanting to wear who i was loud and proud and throwing it all away to conform and try to climb the popularity ladder. and, eventually, like most early teenagers, i tossed away my authenticity and tried to squeeze myself into normalcy.

i wound up hating myself so much. hated my body, hated my personality. hated that i was so smart. hated that boys didn't pay attention to me, hated the popular girls for getting all of the attention. i wanted out of my own skin.

and so i gave 110% of my energy into trying to reinvent myself, a process that would continue on and on for just shy of a couple of decades. desperately tried to lose weight at all costs. molded my personality into one that i thought boys wanted. dumbed myself down so that i would never outshine anyone and draw attention to myself. pleased anyone and everyone because i couldn't deal with people not liking me.

wound up winning "most attractive" in my high school class and thought it was a mistake.

picked a "safe" college major. picked a vanilla career. dated guys who were good on paper.

and then one day i blew up.

who the fuck WAS i? i didn't even know anymore. and after spending years untangling the messy web i wove, i realized it all traced back to that time in my life where i learned at a very young age that society doesn't favor those who go against the grain.

and that made me really angry. because it just isn't true. i NEED to be who i am so that others can feel safe to do so. it's my calling.

so i took time to tend to the festering wound that was my soul screaming out for attention and love. the healing was (and still is) messy. it hurt. it was dark. but i was committed to undoing as much of this crazy self-betrayal as i possibly could.

back to the denver train…

alanis' "thank U" came on and i realized that while i undid so much and reclaimed i'd say 85% of my authenticity, i wasn't giving myself the credit i deserved.

being authentic is hard. reclaiming it after convincing yourself that it's not worth it is even harder. but hearing this song was like a checklist of everything in my life that i had overcome. and it was just incredible.

i broke down and ugly cried and might have given myself half a hug. a hug i so desperately needed.

so, without further ado, please enjoy this overdue moment of owning my awesome:

* * *

i feel like i came out of the womb trying to conquer the world. trying to be the best. killing myself for praise.

bending over backwards just for that quick hit of accomplishment so i could get high, come down, and then quickly realize it wasn't truly satisfying.

truth is, i'm enough when i'm not at my best. i'm enough when i'm broke and in debt. i'm enough when i'm not climbing a ladder of success.

sometimes you need to take a break and just BE. it took me my entire life up to this point to figure that out, but i'm learning to love my state of being-ness. and, ironically, i've never felt more creative.

* * *

i've never been to india, but take all of my spiritual seeking over the years and i might as well have been. things in life have scared me shitless. i'm jaded over a lot. contrary to what i'd like to think, i am capable of being broken. and some of the choices i've made in my life have had consequences that make me want to run screaming in the other direction.

but all of it has contributed to me waking up to who i came to this planet to be.

and sometimes, i need to shut up. externally and internally. stop filling the air with babble and start listening to what's in between the quiet. i'm working on it and it's been a rewarding journey. there is magic in silence. so much.

* * *

i hold grudges. big ones. i'm stubborn, and if you cross me, i don't forget.

i've been working through forgiving because the energy of resentment is just too damn heavy. i've been able to forgive people who've done the unthinkable to me and it's not because i'm being a pushover. selfishly, i don't want the space taking over my brain and heart anymore. so it isn't.

along with forgiveness comes boundaries, and i think this is what a lot of people miss. just because you forgive someone doesn't mean they have to be a part of your life. you can love them from a distance. you can go on with your life and they can go on with theirs, without you ever saying a word.

you deserve the peace that comes with true, deep forgiveness. we all do. and what they don't tell you is that forgiveness is way more for your benefit than for the forgiven party's.

* * *

i've been served a ton of lessons from the universe. like i stopped counting them. there are several main themes though, and a huge one is knowing how to surrender.

just chill out. let it ride. because when you try to control everything, nothing happens. so much nothing happens that it just keeps piling on and next thing you know, you're in a black hole of absolute jack shit nothing.

an amazing thing happens when you let go and jump off the hamster wheel of "show up 24/7" and "try until it hurts". you stop shooting for the future version of yourself and you meet yourself exactly where you're at.

and it's the most humbling thing ever, to know that wherever you are, RIGHT NOW, is enough.

then and only then does the true inspiration come. then and only then can you create honestly and for creation's sake.

i'm right on time, fuckers. and so are you.

* * *

i am finally closing the door on getting off on self-depreciation. on selling myself short. on dimming my light because i care so much about other people, and wanting theirs to shine.

on acting like i don't know enough to make it big. on undervaluing myself. on finding peace in admitting that i didn't take that scary risk i was supposed to take and settled for the one right below it on the list because it's more comfortable. on letting it sink in that we get unlimited chances our entire lives.

i know i'm here on this planet to make a difference. and in embracing what pretty much sounds like my soul screaming at me whenever i do anything that it hates, i remember a little bit more each day why i came.

because crying in the car when a song hits you just right is therapy. because wiping away a flood of tears when you feel so inspired at the future you're scripting out in your head is necessary. because a good sob sesh is actually a most precious human gift.

leave a legacy. start now. live beyond your short time here. you are worthy and you are incredible.

and thank u, alanis. from the bottom of my fragile, awakening, open heart.

let it go*

you are not how shitty your boss makes you feel.
you're not the forgotten items on your to-do list.
you're not the bitch you were in high school.
you aren't the dumb kid your second grade teacher
told you
you were.

you're not fat.
you aren't too bold.
you are not a helpless by-product
of your environment.

you are not your demons
or your darkest secrets.
you are not your past mistakes
or even your
future mistakes.

let
it
go.

you are the universe
experiencing itself with
an infinite number of
possibilities.

you are
what you've been
waiting for.

here's where the story ends

as a kid, i loved being weird. i loved listening to music no one else was listening to. i loved wearing clothes that made me feel good about who i was. i loved making weird art and writing weird fantasy. i devoured weird books and had some of the best, weirdest friends. i truly embraced it.

but then something happened. somewhere between seventh and eighth grade, i made a trade. it seemed like everyone did. there was this sort of divide happening among everyone i knew. people started following trends and becoming obsessed with whatever was popular — popular music, movies, people. and out of this emerged a small group of popular kids. they had the best hair, the prettiest smiles, the newest whatever.

and, all of a sudden, being weird made you a target. you stuck out like a sore thumb and you were either pressured into trying to conform, or you tried to fight the good fight to hang on to your individuality at the cost of being an outsider. some people took that risk and settled into a small group of outsider kids. and while they were the brunt of every joke and constantly bullied, at least they held on to their authenticity. i wonder what that did for them in terms of their development? i'm sure someone's studying that. a research project for another day.

i didn't hold on to my authenticity. i threw it away after a few instances of bullying that i didn't mentally let go of until recently.

in seventh grade, i had a huge crush on a kid, was completely obsessed. i was pretty much obsessed with him forever, actually. forever being from first grade on. over time, he wound up sorting himself into the popular crowd and became more and more out of my reach. one popular girl really liked him too. and she was so pretty, blonde hair, skinny. no acne. i really couldn't compete.

but that didn't stop me from trying to be his seventh-grade girlfriend. i would "ask him out" at the bike rack during recess. he always turned me down. i'd ask him to dance with me at the junior high dances and he'd always say no. and then, eventually, he started dating the popular blonde girl. i mean, of course he did.

and while i was crushed, i didn't stop trying to at least be his friend. this really pissed off popular blonde. pissed her off so much that she came to harass me at my soccer practice with an older, well-known girl bully. they stood at the other side of the fence and started yelling things at me. called me a slut. how could a seventh-grader even BE a slut? i mean, i'm sure they could but i surely wasn't. i didn't understand that though. i cried. my mom came to pick me up and asked me what was wrong. when i told her, she rightfully went into a then extremely embarrassing mom rage and started driving around looking for these girls. we never found them and i was glad. but i was still broken. i started to associate my weirdness with sluttiness, which makes absolutely no sense to adult me, but that's just what happens when you're young.

i gradually started listening to different music, pop music. rap music. r&b.

i made a couple of new friends. we were going to start a girl band. they showed me how to straighten my hair. they had the coolest clothes. i remember one night i was getting ready with them before a school dance and i hated the outfit i had. i asked to borrow some clothes from them and they smirked. they told me i was "too big".

i started a full-blown eating disorder shortly after, at 13 years old. one that would stay with me throughout my twenties. not blaming the entire thing on that one incident, but after recounting all of the little incidents, you can see how they all add up to shaping who you are. who you think you need to be.

i could go on and on with stories like these. i'm sure you have plenty yourself.

we do this weird thing as adults. we grow up and think we've transcended the bullying we were served as kids. but we really don't. not unless we address it. we're taught that trauma comes in the form of big things like rape, abuse, deaths. but the reality is that bullying is traumatic, extremely so. and we carry it through as we grow up, and continue playing out roles based on the wounds we collected as a child. it's both fascinating and terrifying. thankfully, there is a growing body of neo-psychologists starting to cover this kind of thing, so we're trending in the right direction.

for most of my adult life, up until recently, one of my biggest struggles has been trying to express myself authentically. i think i was so wounded from what happened to me as a child that i lost myself. a lot of us do. the trade i made, giving up my authenticity for what was popular, compounded on itself over time and it spit out a version of me that was a total chameleon.

i was like a shapeshifter. i'd change according to who i was around, adapt to my surroundings. i had an office persona. a family persona. a girlfriend persona. i'd sometimes have to do multiple costume changes per day, which was downright exhausting. eventually, my soul told me that i was burning out. from what exactly, i wasn't sure of yet. but i decided to explore it.

what came first from this discovery mission was the realization that my authenticity had become completely compromised. and it hit me like a ton of bricks. i was angry, resentful. confused. annoyed. frustrated. i didn't want to live as a chameleon anymore. i didn't want my weirdness to stay in the closet. i wanted to break free.

but it wasn't that easy. the feeling that so much was at stake by showing the world who i really am was so intense, too big. it was as if me showing up as ME was the biggest risk i could ever take. i am a risk-taker by nature and have done some pretty crazy things in my life, but expressing myself authentically was the one single thing i didn't want to touch.

and i didn't even know HOW. all i knew was that i felt extremely misunderstood. misunderstood for what felt like my entire life.

have you ever encountered sleep paralysis? it's like, this weird thing that happens sometimes, in between waking up from a dream and stepping back into reality. sleep paralysis kind of traps you in between. your eyes are opened, but you can't speak. you try to move your mouth and it feels like you're speaking through glue and mud. and the rest of your body is paralyzed. and it lasts all of a few seconds, but it feels like an eternity.

this is what my being misunderstood felt like. and i had no idea how to cure it. but i was willing to commit to finding out. as soon as i figured out what the diagnosis was, i wanted to undo every single symptom, wanted to get back to who i was. wanted to merge back into my childhood self that was perfectly fine being a weirdo. and admitting that i needed help with this was something i avoided (because i think i can conquer the world by myself — something i'm still working on). i caved, though — thankfully.

i started digging into all kinds of cures for this. self-help books. self-proclaimed authenticity gurus. online seminars. woo-woo spells. tarot cards. podcasts. you name it, i tried it. i wanted to kill the bug that was the inauthenticity virus in my body.

i needed to be done with this story for good. and i needed to figure out that the answer wasn't outside of me.

* * *

i wasn't (and still am not) that well-versed in astrology, but after looking into it some more, i realized that there was more to it than just reading what kind of day i was supposed to be having in the newspaper.

your astro chart really has so much more to offer than just the superficial stuff. a ton more. i'm not the right person to do a deep dive on what yours might have in it, but there are so many great people who speak this language, and if you're interested in filling in the gaps between what you know is wrong with you and how to fix it, i'd definitely recommend you do some astrological spelunking.

the piece of my chart that wound up holding the keys to unlocking my authenticity wasn't anything i've heard of before. it lay in this baby planet/comet ice thing called chiron. never heard of it before, had no idea it existed. it hangs out between saturn and uranus and has an eccentric orbit. and, astrologically, it holds the key to what your greatest wound is. which ironically is also your greatest teacher, and your greatest mission.

my chiron is in the sign of gemini. there's so much i could say about what i uncovered and read, but to make a long story short, my astrological weakness lies in being extremely misunderstood. and not so much ACTUALLY being misunderstood, but more that i constantly worry that people won't understand me.

at first, i felt like i was knocked on my ass. i was pretty

defensive, silently yelling at the articles i was reading, "how DARE you." but it was (and is) true. and it felt like i had just peeked at a blueprint that called out what feels like my biggest struggle. what i knew and experienced was right here in my chart. i couldn't believe it. after i got over the initial shock, i slapped a band-aid on my ego and got to work.

how could i overcome an achilles heel so massive? how could i break free of something that plagued me forever, and was written into some kind of astrological stone? it kind of felt like a hopeless task. i almost felt like it was a sort of playing god to try to go against this shit. as if i could take an eraser and knock out the worst part of my cosmic map.

but i also knew deep within my heart that all wounds are where the light comes in, and that if i could get over this, i could help other people get over this too. the wounds we all come into this world with and the ones we collect on this battleground called life are our greatest opportunities to show our brothers and sisters that we won't go down without a fight. and nine times out of ten, when we fight against the darkest parts of ourselves and come out on top, it's not only a personal victory, but a victory for humanity.

the song that goes with this story is a song by the sundays called "here's where the story ends". to me, it's basically about a woman who's misunderstood, and embarrassed for how she comes off. but she also says over and over through the chorus, "here's where the story ends." this song to me is my stake in the ground against chiron. and every time i want to give up because i'm afraid of being looked at as a nut, i put it on.

i've wanted to write this book for years. i've wanted to help awaken other people but just couldn't find the words, like the sleep paralysis i talked about. i'd sit down to write and what would come out didn't even sound like me. it sounded like everyone else. it sounded like who i THOUGHT was acceptable. because i wasn't.

but the truth is, i am acceptable. i am more than. i am here for a reason, for many reasons. and so are you.

figure out what your ancient inherent wounds are and dance with them. let them teach you. let them light the way to your mission and purpose. because our deepest, most embarrassing flaws are the other side of our greatest, most legendary gifts.

and the world needs all of them.

closer to fine

music has clearly been a driving force in moving me
through my spiritual lessons throughout life. songs and
lyrics have been catalysts for change and beacons of hope.
one of the most beautiful things about this amazing gift
was that, sometimes, the reason why a song was so
important to me wouldn't always immediately reveal itself.
i'd fall madly in love with a song that spoke straight to my
soul, but wouldn't really know why until years later.

and when that moment hits (mostly while i'm driving, and
always followed by an intense crying/laughing fit), it feels
like discovering gold. this has happened to me many times,
and it's always extremely potent. and one of these potent
moments was brought to me by the indigo girls' "closer to
fine".

once i was out of intensive eating disorder treatment in
2007, i transitioned to outpatient and group therapy. the
group therapist actually had us make a mixtape (back then,
i put mine on a CD) of recovery songs. looking back, it's
the most beautiful, poetic, epic-ass foreshadowing of what
i'd eventually go on to create. i was thrilled to bring my
passion for the way music has always moved me into a legit
therapeutic setting. my crazy musical soul language was
validated by a psychologist. totally rad.

there were many songs on that CD, and many of them are
in this book. "closer to fine" stands out to me maybe the

most as the one song that revealed its meaning to me more recently, and while it held a very important message for me when i first decided it was important, the message it gave me later saved my sanity and my life as i knew it.

the song flows through all of the ways we human beings try to make sense of our lives and the world around us. highlights all of the ways we try to figure out why we're here, why we do what we do. how we try to unravel this great mystery called existence.

it calls out our fears, calls out our primal instinct to lean on others when things just aren't adding up. our ever-persistent nature to seek the truth at all costs, or else. it talks about being scrutinized by a doctor. discusses a sort of graduation from a "higher mind" and getting a sort of diploma that signifies a vague freedom. drags us into a late-night bar visit where the singer gets drunk in the name of clarity, only to wake up the next day even more confused and with an added hangover.

and yet, the chorus reminds us that none of this seeking work we do is the real answer. none of it replaces what we already know inside. the less you seek outside of yourself for what defines you, the closer you are to "fine". and while the word "fine" doesn't seem like the best most punch-packing piece of english to use, the way the word is sung in this song lets you know that it's an ephemeral fine. it's the peace that everyone craves. the kind that only comes from deep within.

* * *

when i had my first series of awakening experiences, it threw me into a bit of a spiritual crisis, and this wasn't something unique to me. i found plenty of evidence that it was happening to others and had been happening for as long as there have been humans. but that doesn't make it any less...fucked up.

i was starting to see repeating numbers everywhere, and the frequency at which i'd see them grew by the day. i was able to call the next song up on the radio before hearing it. able to almost read my husband's mind. i felt like i was able to communicate with my dog telepathically. i mean, some fucking weird shit.

and when i started to find answers, everything i would come across would tell me this was part of awakening. that the more conditioning i shed from myself, the more these other little higher self gems would come online. but it still didn't really explain them to me. i was desperate to learn from other people who this had happened to. other people who were ahead of me in this process who weren't in a mental institution. because although i'm crazy in a lot of ways, i knew that these "crazy" things that were happening to me were not at all crazy. they felt like they belonged to me, like second nature. but that wasn't enough for me. i needed some external validation.

i started connecting with people who i felt "got it". people i looked up to from a distance and wanted to get to know. some of these people were amazing and i am still in touch with today, and some eventually revealed themselves to me as phony. but the phoniness is extremely hard to spot.

think of it this way: you know you want to learn japanese, but you can't speak it at all. would you be able to tell the difference between someone speaking fluent, perfect japanese and someone who just sounds like they are? i wouldn't. and this happens with so many other things. especially in the arena of spiritual teachers. and it's so risky because when you cross over into the spiritual realm of knowledge, you can't really back it up with science or hard credibility, because it's heavily suppressed and hidden from us on purpose. i mean, would the powers that be want everyone to know that they're actual superheroes? we wouldn't need them anymore.

so how do you know if someone is a good person to learn from or not? you have to trust your intuition. you have to use discernment. you have to get really good at trusting those bad feelings you get when someone says something that rubs you the wrong way. you have to become best friends with that nag in your soul that's telling you to peace the fuck out. you have to be willing to bet on yourself, that you already know the answers.

but this is way easier said than done.

throughout our entire lives, we've been led to believe that we can't find answers unless we ask someone for them. unless someone with authority tells us what's true. unless someone with X degree from Y university writes a paper on it. unless joe schmo reporter from CNN confirms it actually happened. and this ruins us. the intuition we are born with gradually erodes away until we're completely dependent on what's outside of us.

this gets us into trouble. and it got me into major trouble at one point in my quest for spiritual truth. i bounced from teacher to teacher, looking for the answers to why i was here. what i was supposed to be doing, my mission. i wanted to know so i could get the fuck to work. i was all good with leaving my old life behind, i just needed someone to tell me what was next. i was tired of being in limbo and was going broke in the process of finding myself. i was running out of gas.

with every teacher i'd find, i'd lose a part of myself. i felt like i was losing touch with the people around me, finding it harder and harder to relate to those i loved so much. and while inside i felt like something was wrong, one teacher told me that everything was right. that i wasn't supposed to fit in anymore. that i had to leave everything behind, including myself. ditch my personality. trade my current life for a higher one that they told me was the only way.

the nag that i had in my soul wouldn't give up. i started to become physically ill from ignoring it, from continuing to seek. until i eventually reached a critical point where i had to break away and stop seeking altogether. it was extremely difficult, because breaking away would mean that i wasn't closer to figuring out the answers. confusion set in, and a ton of heartbreak and disappointment.

my seeking broke me. the very thing that i thought was going to lead me to peace and clarity and a higher life led me to a really dark place.

but after letting myself grieve, i realized that while my seeking led me down a crazy destructive path, it created a new relationship with my intuition that was more powerful than any teacher i had ever come across. i started trusting those nags more and more. started feeling all of the different ways they'd hit me, i learned their language. i started believing in my own internal GPS system. with every decision i made while following it, i earned more points. i unlocked a superpower that ironically was with me the entire time.

the less i looked outside of myself for answers, and the more that i trusted my instincts, the closer i was to feeling sane. the closer i was to "fine".

* * *

seeking is a very important part of awakening. everyone does it, and to an extent, it's necessary. the danger lies in when your seeking leads you to a place where you put your own experiences and life in the hands of someone else. this can really mess you up big time. but on the flip side, a positive thing that comes out of seeking is that you get to really work your discernment muscles. the soul nags really start to light up inside you, gut feelings you may have never felt before.

and i think it's the fucking coolest thing ever. it's like the universe knows that the true knowledge of awakening has been hidden from us, so it throws in a little personal compass to help you figure things out. it's the ultimate earth game hack.

when i heard "closer to fine" more recently, it all became clear to me. spiritual seeking is kind of like trying to put two same-sided magnets together. the more you try to connect them, the more they push apart. because that's not the point of magnets. they're supposed to fit with their complement.

at some point, you realize that you have everything you need inside of you, and your seeking meets you there and it just fits, it clicks. it happens to everyone on the awakening path. and once you get it, it's like something else unlocks and you're able to help other people get it. and if this is you, maybe you'll come up with a better analogy for this than magnets.

to drive it all home, seek to find what you need to find, but don't sell out to someone else's prescribed method of awakening. reality check: it doesn't exist. sure, we have lists of common things that occur, and people's accounts of what happens, but no one other than YOU can walk you through your own awakening. a good guide will let you figure out things on your own and just be there for you as a sounding board. they'll never discount your experiences, or tell you that you need to get away from your family, or that you're now in some new level of human existence where people can't even see you anymore (yeah, that's actually out there. stay AWAY from that shit). an even better guide will celebrate your progress and be completely transparent when they're no longer needed. because it's about YOU, not them.

and if you ever need a reminder that you're always closer to fine than you think, listen to the indigo girls.

rainbow

i don't really care for country music. i pretty much hated it and wrote it off as shallow and annoying for most of my life, but i'm changing my mind. i can't believe just how much heart and soul and power i missed by not giving it a chance. and for that, i thank kacey musgraves.

the first time i heard "rainbow", i was sitting in a hair and makeup chair, getting done up for the talk i was going to do while at the public-speaking training mentioned in the thank u story. i asked the makeup artist what the song was since i never heard it before and she was like, "oh it's kacey musgraves". never heard of her, didn't even realize it was country.

and when i first heard "rainbow" i didn't hear the lyrics or remember them, just the title and the raw piano and kacey's sweet, pure voice. it hit something in me that i didn't know was there. it hit me in the way that a song hits you and makes you remember something deep inside, something you tucked away and forgot about, probably on purpose. i filed it away and then i had to go on stage, and i left "rainbow" in the dressing room.

i didn't hear it again until months later.

after i got home from the training, i felt so lost. i was so sick and tired of chasing these dreams of mine that were half-baked. tired of spending money i didn't have in the name of self-development. tired of having the most bipolar relationship with every single GREAT IDEA i had.

starting and stopping and creating and scrapping and over and over and over. i hated everything.

i left my job under the impression that i'd become a self-made millionaire conveniently timed with when my personal loan ran out. all i had to do was manifest it. light candles every morning, meditate. ask the universe for what the fuck i'm here for. and then wait until my million dollar idea mission plan showed up.

and i thought it showed up so many times. and every time i thought it did, i was wrong. but didn't find out i was wrong until i put another dent in my credit card. another ten thousand dollars i didn't have, gone. and another breakthrough i thought i was having, straight down the drain.

time was ticking. money literally pouring out of me with no end in sight. i eventually became hopeless. went into a really dark place mentally. how could i know so deeply that i had to leave that shit job to become who i was supposed to be, but not get handed a game plan? where was the new hire orientation? where were the instructions? the trainings? the mentors? the guaranteed formula for success?

there wasn't one.

and so the day i heard "rainbow" again, i was in my car and listened to the lyrics for the first time. and the flood gates opened.

there was kacey again, crooning away in the most angelic way. piercing my beat-up heart. wrapping up my broken soul in a warm blanket that just came out of the dryer. i almost had to pull over.

plain and simple, the song is about a storm. except the storm is over. but the person she's singing to doesn't realize that the rain had stopped. the person she's singing to is still all raincoat and boots and umbrella and has no fucking clue. still storming through even though there's now clear skies and a rainbow.

everything is alright.

i felt like a fucking insane person, caught up in my own shit storm of surmounting problems i had no solutions to. caught up in this cycle of shelling out money to buy my way into my purpose. i just wanted to pay someone to give it to me. and unfortunately, i didn't learn after the first time. or the second. or the third. $45,000 later, i hit a wall that the universe decided to create for me. a literal financial boundary that i now live on the edge of every single day.

it's terrible. it's a crippling pain that i can't even explain.

so much shame and guilt, and god, just like…a terrible feeling that i'm some kind of irresponsible person who doesn't have their shit together.

and so much anger. anger that it shouldn't be this hard. that it shouldn't be a struggle and a war to figure out what you're on this planet to do. it's unfair that people who take risks and say "fuck you" to the man are quickly punished for their decisions. laughed at by society for not being able to hack it. looked at like some flighty idiot free spirit who will eventually wind up back in a cubicle like everyone else who tries to leave does. when i was recruiting, i'd interviewed several people with resume gaps, and when asked they told me they had "gone out on their own" and had a business. and then whenever i would ask them about it, they'd always have the same reaction. they'd break eye contact with me and look down and tell me it didn't work out. and then we would look at each other again and share the ever so slightest, subtle mental hug, quickly broken by a "and now i'm here! talking to you!"

i didn't want to be that person. i'm not going to be that person. i'm going to get out of my own way and fucking figure it out.

except that the same approach to my career before i left doesn't apply to your purpose. you don't hustle your way to the top of your purpose. you don't schmooze other people until they give it to you because there are no people and if there were, they wouldn't have it. you don't go to school for your purpose and get a certificate at the end that lets everyone know you're qualified.

there is no playbook. you have to make it yourself. and that is a downright awful conclusion. i didn't want to accept it.

historically, i'm not someone who fails. i push and push and push until i get what i want. always have, my entire life. anything i wanted, i got. any hole i crawled into, i dug out. came out better. resilient. untouchable.

but now i was failing. a lot. and pretty badly.

so many announcements on social media. so many failed launches. so many coaches and workshops and spiritual books and online courses and rituals and sage and binaural beats. but no success. not a single drop. only embarrassing and awkward conversations and debt. a lot of debt.

and so i let kacey sing to me in my car that day. i let myself cop to the fact that the fucking storm i was in was created by me. i was suiting up every day, hitting the world up to see what shit it was going to throw at me next. i'd walk straight into the self-created wind, umbrella blowing backwards and turning inside out, getting just completely obliterated by my own hell.

i needed a way out. i want a way out. i don't want to do this anymore. this is a roller-coaster i'm done riding. i need off this hamster wheel before it kills me. before i kill me. because the truth of the matter is, my soul isn't a storm at all. my higher self is a ray of light, filling me up every single minute i decide to tune in. it's in the clarity i get when i'm meditating. the stillness out in nature when no one else is around. in my husband's hugs, in my dog's sleepy cuddles. in the colors of the rainbow of possibilities this life has for me.

and i can't see them if i'm constantly worrying about the storm. it just doesn't work that way. it's so counter-intuitive.

to be able to hear what you're supposed to do next, you need to stop. and i mean fucking stop to a screeching halt. for more than a day. way more. you need to completely stop TRYING. and who does that today? we're not taught to stop. we have to keep going. keep running. keep learning and showing up and go go go GO. until you get what you want. because THAT'S modern success, baby.

but it's not soul success.

the search for soul success isn't cheap labor. it's expensive. it will cost you your old life. cost you everything you thought you knew. cost you your sanity, your emotional stability. and it never ends. you listen until things make sense and then they don't and you have to start up again. over and over and over.

and you can't be comfortable in it unless you surrender. unless you accept the unknown and that there's nothing you can do about it. you have to be OK with going broke if that's what it takes. you have to risk everything. because once you give into the call, it doesn't leave you alone. it burns and stings and gnaws at you. it shakes you in the middle of the night when you just want to get some fucking sleep, for christ's sake.

i'm at the point now where i finally listened to kacey. my boat's tied up, i'm not in rain gear. i'm sitting in the humid misty aftermath, looking at the rainbow. not really totally believing it's real yet, but i see it. and i'm done struggling in the sense that i'm really trying not to create any additional storms.

i have no idea what i'm doing and that's my new existence. i am learning to trust in the fact that i'm on the right path, even if it feels like i have a blindfold on. and it is so much lighter, so much easier. i am cutting myself a break for how i had to get to this point. and that it wrecked me financially. i have no idea what's going to happen, but i am trusting that i am being taken care of. i surrender every day and give it all to the universe. and it pays me in clarity.

it pays me with a warm sense that everything is alright now. a pat on the back that i'm not a failure, in fact, i'm doing everything right. i'm doing what most people fear the most. i'm living my truth, literally no matter the cost. and if this is how the rest of my life is going to be, i'm fine with that.

i am learning to be OK with uncertainty. i don't welcome it yet, but i let it in to have a look around while i follow it around at a distance and make sure it doesn't steal anything. and every day it stays a little while longer. i'm cautiously optimistic, heavy on the optimism. knowing i came here with a mission is all i need to know. that's the only prerequisite any of us need to start.

and i hope you do start, despite it all. i hope you jump in regardless of what happens after you do. and when you jump, i hope you go all in. because even if you can't feel it, you are held. the net was laid out for you the day you were born and it's so tired of going unused. your life is so much more than the mundane. your soul didn't come here to experience that, and on a deep level, you know.

trust the knowing. it will all be way more than alright.

imagine this*

imagine this scenario:

say that before you were born,
your soul is hanging out up in the universe and
you're getting kinda bored.
you're like,
"i love it up here and all, but eternity
is a really long time."

so you check out this assignment you heard about.
apparently it's all the rage.

you're allowed to go to a planet called
EARTH
to have a chance to take everything that's amazing about
you
and help turn it around because
wow, it's one clusterfuck of a mess.

your mission is to use the small amount of
human years you're allotted to make
the biggest impact you can.
the catch?

you have to come back to earth as a baby.
a blank slate.
you don't remember anything about your mission
at all.
oh, and
you're also wrapped up in a whole side drama

made up of your
family
race
class
general life circumstances, etc.
that the universe picks for you
just to keep things interesting.

think:
the hardest obstacle course plus
the toughest video game plus
the most difficult reality game survival show
ever.

oh yeah,
not to mention that
because of how messed up earth is nowadays,
the odds are really ummm,
NOT in your favor.

if your time runs out during this earth assignment
and you don't remember why you're there,
you'll keep coming back
as a baby
and repeat the process until you figure it out.

you could potentially be leaving your cushy,
magical universe eternal dream life behind
for a massive portion of your
cosmic existence.
you'd very likely be caught up in
eons
of a suffering mess.

but in the off chance you DO remember?
congratulations.
you've just unlocked the greatest prize known to man.
your rewards
and possibilities
will be endless.

so,
would you take the assignment?
how would your life change if you lived like you did?

(or maybe you're smiling
at this page
because you know
you already did.)

about the author

Natalie Windle Fell is an author, system buster, and all-around truth seeker. In 2018, Natalie quit her corporate job without a backup plan and dedicated her attention to her own awakening and helping others along the path. She loves cooking, art in all forms, and off-color humor. Natalie currently lives in Philadelphia with her husband and rambunctious Pomeranian.

instagram @nataliewindlefell

www.nataliewindlefell.com

CPSIA information can be obtained
at www.ICGtesting.com
Printed in the USA
BVHW040403020321
601389BV00005B/846